Take a Quality Ride

Take a Quality Ride

The Realities of Implementing a Quality Management System

Susan M. Hinkle

iUniverse, Inc.
New York Lincoln Shanghai

Take a Quality Ride
The Realities of Implementing a Quality Management System

iUniverse books may be ordered through booksellers or by contacting:

iUniverse
2021 Pine Lake Road, Suite 100
Lincoln, NE 68512
www.iuniverse.com
1-800-Authors (1-800-288-4677)

ISBN-13: 978-0-595-40194-9 (pbk)
ISBN-13: 978-0-595-84570-5 (ebk)
ISBN-10: 0-595-40194-5 (pbk)
ISBN-10: 0-595-84570-3 (ebk)

Printed in the United States of America

Contents

Acknowledgements

I would like to extend acknowledgement and gratitude to the following persons for their exceptional participation, support, and encouragement in the publication of this book:

Kristine Titzer, Director of IT Consulting Services
Richard Bechtold, PhD, President, Abridge Technology
Joanne O'Leary, CMMI Lead Appraiser
William Laramie, CIO, Triumph Technologies, Inc.
Gloria Redman, President and CEO, Triumph Technologies, Inc.

I would like to thank the staff at Triumph Technologies, Inc. for their undying enthusiasm. I would also like to express my gratitude to my Uncle Dominic for his pearls of wisdom and colorful euphemisms, Tyric Sims, President, Facet Technologies for his strength and outlook, Mark Smith, Asset Manager, Triumph Technologies, Inc. for his interminable wit, and Rich Neufang for being there for me. A special thank you goes to Christopher Hall, Quality Engineer, Triumph Technologies, Inc. and Amy Webber, Customer Service Specialist, Triumph Technologies for their extraordinary patience and dedication to the cause.

Author photograph by W. Laramie, you are an artist!

Susan M. Hinkle

Preface

For many small organizations, the time, effort, cost, and culture shock associated with implementing a Quality Management System can be overwhelming. With that in mind, I am hoping to share some of my successes so you can borrow some of the ideas, and identify some of the pitfalls I encountered so you can avoid them. The intent of this book is to explain the realities of what you could encounter when implementing a Quality Management System and to discuss the things the other books on how to implement a Quality Management System and consultants might not necessarily tell you. This book is intended for use by small commercial and government organizations outside the realms of Information Technology (IT), software development and systems engineering.

There are numerous reasons why small organizations are eager to implement a Quality Management System. Adherence to Quality Management System requirements can result in decreased costs, increased schedule predictability, improved product quality, increased customer satisfaction, and a positive return on investment according to studies.

Many government agencies require Capability Maturity Model Integration (CMMI) compliance to be eligible to compete on certain contracts. Unfortunately, few small organizations that start down the road toward implementation ever reach their goal. Studies conducted by the Software Engineering Institute have shown that organizations with little experience in process improvement projects typically require eighteen to twenty four months to reach CMMI Level 2.

Many books out there explain systematically the "How to" for implementing different Quality Management Systems. The purpose of this book is to tell you what consultants and other publications may not tell you, and that is the realities of what you may encounter and what you can expect when implementing a Quality Management System. This book is from my (the author's) perspective and personal experience in implementing Quality Management Systems in various industries over a 16-year career span. Bear in mind that these are only my experiences, and in your specific industry or your specific Quality Management System that you choose to implement, the results, expectations or realities may be somewhat different. A couple of years ago after a successful CMMI implementation, I was asked by the senior management staff of the company that I was working for to write down how I implement, how I do this successfully every time. The timing just was not right at that point in time for me to write anything down or for me to explain the intricacies of implementing a Quality Management System. Nevertheless, as time wore on, I was seeing that most of the companies and/or government agencies that were trying to attain a CMMI rating or ISO registrations were faced with roadblocks and hitting speed bumps during their implementation projects. As a result, it affected their success when it came to implementing the Quality Management Systems they were trying to implement quickly and effectively. So I thought, "Well, maybe it's because they had no real concept, no real idea of what they could expect, therefore, they couldn't plan for it." The realities of what you may truly encounter when implementing a Quality Management System are what this book is about. Having realistic ideas upfront with regard to what you can expect during an implementation will enable you to plan for potential issues.

Chapter One

The Quality Management System

A Quality Management System is a network of interconnected processes. Each process uses resources to turn inputs into outputs and all of these processes are interconnected by means of an input/output relationship. Each process generates at least one output, and this output becomes an input for another process. These input/output relationships glue all the processes together. That is what makes it a system.

A primary concern of any organization is the quality of its products and services. Many times, specific quality requirements are stated in organizational objectives. A Quality Management System should be developed and implemented for the purpose of accomplishing the objectives set out in the organization's strategic and business objectives. This book focuses on the realities of implementing a Quality Management System in accordance with ISO®, the Project Management Institute's Project Management Body of Knowledge® (PMBOK®) and CMMI[SM] Methodologies.

Implementing a Quality Management System is similar to going on a ride at the theme park. Take for example, a roller coaster. You are at a theme park with friends and the group wants to try out the new roller coaster. The one that you have heard so much about that has corkscrews goes upside down, and backwards.

You think to yourself, "What happened to the regular roller coasters…the roller coasters that I went on when I was a kid?" Deep down you know you have to go on the ride with your friends that have been pressuring you or be left behind.

In the case of business, the market or the industry is bearing pressure for you to implement a Quality Management System. In many cases, having a Quality Management System implemented has become a requirement to do business. But you are apprehensive—why? Because it is kind of scary, you have never been on a ride like that. You have heard stories about it, both good and bad. You do not know how safe it is going to be for you or in the case of business, for your organization. What kinds of changes will this mean for you? How much money is it going to cost? What is it going to do to the structure of things and the organizational culture? You end up standing in line for what seems like forever, while these thoughts and questions roll around in your head, and the anxiety builds and builds. Things are just getting started!

Then, you get on the ride, you are sitting in the roller coaster car and they lock you in so now you know you have to go through with it. You are committed to the ride. You have an investment already because you have been standing in line for what seems like an interminable amount of time. The car starts to move. Everyone around you is excited. They do not know what to expect and they are anxious. There are some people that just do not want to be there, you can tell by the look on their faces, but like you, they felt the pressure from their friends. You start inching up that hill, the very first hill on the rollercoaster, and it seems like it is taking forever as you keep going higher and higher and your anxiety keeps building and building.

You finally get to the top. As you look down, there is so much air and you are up so high! You start down the other side, and it goes amazingly fast. You find yourself being thrown back and forth and lurched around. People in the car are screaming and their hands are in the air, but oddly enough, they are smiling, laughing, and having fun. It occurs to you that the ride is not all that bad! You continue to twist and turn on the ride and just as things are getting really fun, you come to the end. The ride has gone faster than you thought it would. It just seemed endlessly long in the beginning. You realize when you step off the ride that going through all of that was actually not as awful as you imagined. Surprisingly enough, you find yourself getting in line to do it all over again!

When implementing a Quality Management System in an organization that doesn't have a formal system in place, you may find that initially everyone will think it's a great idea, and they may say, "Oh yes, we've got to do this. It is great for business. It will be great for the organization." Management has mandated that a Quality Management System will be implemented. Things start happening, but slowly, very slowly, and in the beginning there seems to be little progress.

Processes and procedures are being documented and people are suddenly being held accountable, especially now that you are collecting data for metrics. There are always people in the organization that will embrace the implementation, embrace the changes, and be very cooperative, but more often than not in the beginning, people will be resistant. You may start to hear people say, "We never had to do it this way before and everything has been fine." or "Why?" or "This is extra work for me, when am I supposed to find the time to do it?"

You will probably find that you will hear the same types of common excuses throughout the organization and throughout the various layers in the organization from executives all the way down to the line staff. Excuses as to why they cannot engage in implementing the Quality Management System…or why it would not work and why it is too much or too hard. But you will also find that eventually you will have some small victories on the way up that hill. You will make a rather small change that makes somebody's job a little easier and that person will realize the change was not that hard and, no, it did not take a significant amount of extra time. This will result in successive, small victories. Eventually, by the time you get to the top of that roller coaster, you will have had enough small victories to where most of your staff is on board and engaged in the implementation. That is when you can actually start to experience the fun of the ride.

Chapter Two

Types of Quality Management Systems

Understanding the basis from which Quality Management Systems originated provides you a good start but it is only the beginning. Can you feel the pull of gravity as you begin to ascend the first hill of the roller coaster? As with any system, there are levels and degrees of design. This chapter will discuss the types of Quality Management Systems and what you will need to do as you begin to outline what it is you desire your Quality Management System to achieve for you, your organization and most importantly your customers.

<u>Define Your Needs and Requirements</u>

It is critical to define your needs and/or requirements and the results you expect from implementing a Quality Management System. On average, organizations go into implementation with very different expectations for the outcome. Organizations might go into the implementation thinking that they can buy a 'canned', packaged software, or they will hire a consultant to come in and just put the systems and processes in place and believe that the system will work. A Quality Management System that is 'put in place' will not work. Without the buy in from your employees, and a highly visible commitment from the organization's executive management team, you are doomed to failure. A canned, bought and paid for consultant's system will not sustain itself, nor is it realistic. In order to make a Quality Management System work within an organization and benefit the organization to really get that true and realistic return on investment, organizations must understand that it will only work when absolutely all staff is fully engaged in the project. The way to become fully engaged is for absolutely everyone in the organization to participate in varying degrees, in the development and implementation of the system.

Employee ownership of a program or effort can only be achieved if employees are involved and responsible for the success of the effort. As you define your needs and requirements you must have the ideas and suggestions of the employees, after all your employees are the ones who will make the system work or standby and watch it die. The only way to have an effective system is to spend the time defining the requirements and communicating the advantages and whys of your implementation to the entire organization's workforce.

Types of Quality Management Systems

There are several different types of Quality Management Systems, industry and product specific, examples of which are TL 9000, which is for telecommunications, QS 9000, which is for the automotive industry and API-Q1, American Petroleum Institute, which is specific for the Petroleum, Petrochemical and Natural Gas Industry. Another industry-specific Quality Management System is ASME NQA-1, which is specific to the nuclear industry. There are also nonspecific Quality Management Systems, such as ISO 9000, which is more general and internationally recognized.

Then there are systems such as CMMI, Capability Maturity Model Integration, which is not technically a standard, but for implementation purposes, it can be considered as such. The Software Engineering Institute (SEI) deems CMMI as a 'model' rather than a standard, however, to gain a maturity level rating or capability level rating, either you comply or you do not comply with the model.

Standard: A set of criteria (some of which may be mandatory), voluntary guidelines, and best practices. A basis for comparison; a reference point against which other things can be evaluated

Model: A representation of a set of components of a process, system, or subject area, generally developed for understanding, analysis, improvement, and/or replacement of the process. A representation of information, activities, relationships, and constraints.

CMMI was originally commissioned by the U.S. Department of Defense (DoD) to help them qualify software vendors' capabilities. United States government organizations, especially the DoD, mainly use organizations' CMMI status as a gating mechanism to exclude non-certified organizations from bidding on contracts. As a result, most of the contactors for the DoD and the U.S. federal government have achieved or are trying to achieve some level of CMMI compliance. Approximately 80% of the U.S. organizations that performed SCAMPI v1.1 appraisals are the DoD, the federal government, and their contractors. CMMI is typically specific to performing work with or for the government.

When choosing a Quality Management System, you need to define your needs and requirements as well as the expected results. As such, you should look at the industry that you are in, the products or services that you produce, and what is going to benefit your organization's future growth and sustaining that growth.

Richard Bechtold, President of Abridge Technology, decided on implementing CMMI "mostly as a function of our specific business needs." He stated that, "Software development is a key part of what we do, so I wanted to start with a quality model that was specifically designed for use by software organizations. We started with the Software Capability Maturity Model, and later transitioned to the Capability Maturity Model Integration. Our Quality Management System resulted from interpreting these models to better achieve our business objectives." Mr. Bechtold also indicated that, "For the majority of the client organizations I've supported in implementing Quality Management Systems, their decision when selecting a Quality Management System was based upon current or anticipated contract opportunities. In particular, here in the Washington D.C. area, if some type of quality standard compliance language is included in Requests for Proposals/Tenders (especially as a pre-condition, but also as an evaluation criteria) organizations became hugely motivated (that is to say, executive management became quite focused on quality system implementation and standards or model compliance) and they identified and adopted one or more quality standards as appropriate."

Implementing ISO and/or CMMI

For the purposes of this book and for the targeted audience, two different systems will be referenced, ISO 9000, which is internationally recognized and is a standard, and CMMI, the Capability Maturity Model Integration, which is more specific to government agencies and contracts and is a model. More often than not, government contractors will opt to implement CMMI due to requirements within Request for Proposals (RFPs) or Request for Quotations (RFQs). According to studies done by the SEI, approximately 80 percent of all government contracts being released, require some sort of CMMI level rating. As a result, most government contractors are choosing to go with CMMI. However, more often than not, contractors combine it with an already existing ISO 9000 Quality Management System or they will decide to implement ISO 9000 afterwards.

The key is to choose the right Quality Management System at the right time. Which Quality Management System should you implement first? It depends. What will benefit your organization the most? Some organizations choose to implement ISO 9000 only, some opt for CMMI, and some choose both. In a case where an organization chooses to implement both, I almost always opt for implementing an ISO Quality Management System first and then piggyback CMMI into the ISO system to fill in any holes that may exist. Unfortunately, with the case of most government contracts, the requirement is there for CMMI, and time and money are of the essence. Therefore, it is not surprising that most organizations choose to implement CMMI first. If you find that you must implement CMMI first, the use of alternative practices gives you the latitude to be able to effectively implement ISO after CMMI.

For Kristine Titzer, Director of IT Consulting Services, the logical choice for her organization was to implement CMMI. "The Quality Management System had to support the strategic direction of the organization and the requirements of current programs/contracts."

Because the Software Engineering Institute developed CMMI for the Department of Defense, it was originally intended for use in systems engineering and software development environments. Those organizations that are trying to implement CMMI which provide services outside the realm of IT have a much more difficult task at hand. It is very possible, however, to implement CMMI for service organizations by the use of alternative practices. "We chose CMMI because we felt that it was appropriate for the way our company operates," said Gloria Redman, CEO of Triumph Technologies. "It is the best fit and we needed processes internally with or without a certification. We need the processes to be able to be competitive in our environment. The certification is icing on the cake and we are very pleased to have a CMMI rating. We chose CMMI because it has a direct relationship to the processes that affect the type of business we do with the government and overall, it is the most flexible for us. The implementation of CMMI has allowed us to really hone in on the strengths that we have as a company and that allows us to provide our clients with the best solutions."

When posed the question of what Quality Management System did you choose and how did you come to that decision, William Laramie, CIO of Triumph Technologies said, "As a government contractor providing IT services, we evaluated the government requirements being levied on contractors pursuing work in both DoD and DHS, and realized that in order to remain competitive we would need to become compliant with CMMI standards. In addition, we believed that the processes and procedures driven by the CMMI model would be beneficial to improving the internal operations within the organization."

These recurring themes drive most business decisions: competitive edge, maintaining industry practices and standards and streamlining business practices. The title or name of the system does not matter. What matters most is having repeatable and sustainable processes and procedures that assure products and/or services are delivered in a consistent manner. i.e., with the highest quality possible.

In summary, we discussed setting the foundation for your decision making regarding your Quality Management System by defining your needs and your requirements, and talking about some types of Quality Management Systems. I will now discuss what many organizations consider the most critical decision you may face, the make or buy decision. It can very well be the decision that most influences the success or failure of your implementation.

Chapter Three

The Make or Buy Decision

Money, time, and ownership of the system—these are some items that you need to consider when trying to decide whether to bring in a consultant versus tackling the implementation of a Quality Management System within your organization.

The first decision point to consider: *money.* If you develop and implement internally, the cost would be significantly less than hiring a consultant. Typically, when working with a consultant, you will get guidance and that is what you are paying for, their guidance. Your own staff will inevitably do the actual work of documenting all of your processes and procedures then implementing those systems. Therefore, in addition to actually paying a consultant for the guidance, you end up doing much of the real work internally using your own resources. Consultants are not typically going to do the work for you unless you buy those services as well. It has been my experience that when you engage a consultant, you are signing up for a set amount of services. During the development process, other services that you may need or other assistance that you may need will inevitably crop up that are not included in the general agreement, which means that it will end up costing you considerably more.

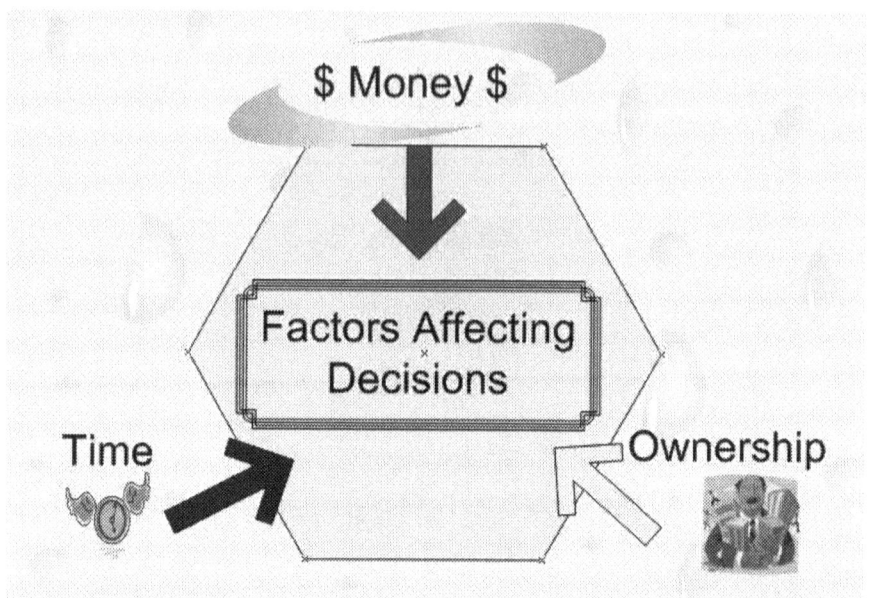

When asked about the make or buy decision for her organization Gloria Redman said, "We conducted a survey of the environment based on companies we knew that were pursuing CMMI plus looking on the internet to see what was being offered. We discovered a company that had an outstanding quality person and we felt to really put the program into effect, that is where we needed to start. So we based our approach on finding the right people and then using that person to develop a quality system within the company and using that approach to maintain a good company and a quality service and a quality company to help us."

With regard to time, obviously consultants are in business to make money. So they may not have your timeframe at the forefront of their agenda. In other words, if you set a timeframe, "We would like to have this Quality Management System developed and implemented within 12 months," you may not, and in most cases *will not*, get the momentum going that you need because consultants are not there day-to-day, eight hours a day working with you, thus affecting your timeline. In order for consultants to do that, you could pay for it and it would probably cost a substantial amount of money. Richard Bechtold noted that, "After a decade of providing support for Quality Management System implementations, not a single client has relied exclusively on consulting support. Every one has assigned internal resources to conduct implementation. Most of the time I'm used as a consultant—which is exactly how it should be—and not as an implementer."

Let us pause for a moment and dispel the common perception that every Quality Management System implementation is more or less the same. No, it is not! Making a Quality Management System work in an organization is all about making it relevant and real to that organization. Therefore, you need to watch out for the consulting company that wants to sell you their "one size fits all" solution typically known as the "cookie cutter approach." More often than not, this has led to systems that are not sufficiently relevant or appropriate to the organization in which they have been implemented. Creating generic procedures that are lengthy and not related to your business processes will only lead to frustration and extra cost of maintenance. However, common templates can be useful as a means to provide some direction. In many large organizations, they have also been used to establish a common framework with aligned processes. If a consultant is able to help you link your activities, products and services then your system can take shape as a tool that is able to support management in making the right decisions at the right time. When asked about the 'make or buy' decision, Kristine Titzer stated that,

> We used an outside consultant for Quality Management System implementation assessment (ISO and CMMI), but not for system implementation itself. We wanted a system that was tailored to our organization and as easy as possible to follow. Only someone that worked in the organization could provide that perspective.

With regard to doing it yourself, yes, you can utilize internal resources and therefore end up cutting your time down to implementation because everyone is engaged. A consultant does not take ownership of the system. A consultant may build a system for you or assist you in building your system, but actually understanding the inner workings of the system and really owning the system is still left to you. This means that if you only have a few of your people involved with the consultant in building the system, not everyone in the organization will be engaged. If you build the system yourself, more of your staff, if not everyone, would be engaged in building the system, therefore they would own it. The more the executive management team and employees have been involved in the implementation process, the more the system is used. The executive management team is more satisfied with the results, and quality improvements will continue after certification or registration is achieved. Important factors for successful implementation are the attitude of the organization when the implementation starts, and detailed and accountable plans (i.e. who is going to do what, by when and how will the actions be reported back through the organization to the primary point of contact for implementation). Lastly and crucial for the highest organizational impact, the documentation that is developed must be adapted to the business both for strategic objectives and tactical maximization. Many Quality Management Systems have gone to an early grave simply because the employees rejected the system as steeped in bureaucracy with no apparent relevancy or benefit to helping them with their specific jobs.

> We believed that it was crucial to own the processes and procedures. We started out by evaluating service vendors in CMMI practices but were not satisfied with what appeared to be a cookie cutter approach to installing ready-made processes and procedures with little regard to tailoring for the needs of the organization. We feared that without an organization wide buy-in we would have a system on paper and this is not what we wanted. As a result, we opted to recruit a proven performer to work as an employee of the organization to implement the program. In hiring a person, we gained an employee who would work from within the organization to adapt the culture to embrace the quality program. This effort has led to streamlined processes and procedures that are repeatable and sustainable, observed William Laramie.

A little over a year ago, I recall listening to a consultant's pitch for the services they were offering with regard to developing and implementing CMMI. They had several slides in their presentation, but none of the slides actually offered any significant detail. Throughout the presentation, I asked questions such as "Are you saying that you will assist in implementing the configuration management system? Where no systems exist, are you proposing to develop and implement them? Does that include software? Who is going to implement it?" As the presentation wore on, I continued to have similar questions, requesting more information and detail, none of which could be answered. Their presentation indicated that we would have a Return on Investment (ROI) of 7:1, but when asked to quantify the claim, they could not do it. Basically, they did not have answers for very key questions that were critical when deciding whether to use a consultant or not. If you are a small organization, it may be helpful to use a consultant for guidance purposes and to map out an appropriate project plan for a successful implementation. If you are a large organization and can afford to pay for all that guidance, the additional tools, and the additional cost to have a consultant come in and set the system up for you, then that might be the way to go. The decision is yours, just be well informed.

There are elements that are similar with each implementation I have done, regardless of industry or the type of system. When I implement a Quality Management System for an organization, I try to go into it, customizing everything I do for that industry and that particular organization and their products and/or services. You do not want to bring in a consultant that has a 'one size fits all' version of a system that would require you to have to institute change within your organization in order to make *your* processes fit *their* system. That is not cost effective, and could be detrimental to your business. The ultimate objective of the implementation of a Quality Management System is to enhance activities and processes already in existence and to interject a system that will provide consistent and reliable workflow and output of your products or services.

As I stated before, the make or buy decision is in fact going to be about money, time, and ownership of the system. If you are considering a consultant, then you must assess what the consultant's agenda is. Is the consultant simply making another sale or is he committed to assisting you become successful in your endeavor? Large organizations can usually utilize their own personnel when implementing quality initiatives, which is not always the case for smaller organizations. The current downsizing trend has unleashed into the marketplace a plethora of external consultants whose sole focus appears to be "helping" small businesses become registered or certified to the ISO 9000 or CMMI. Many small organizations hire and rely on these external consultants. Unfortunately, they may discover along the way that the consultant does not understand the organization's business, products or services, or processes, resulting in a documented system that has little or no merit. There are many exceptional consultants available. They may come into your organization, take a look at your existing system and the way that you do things, assist you in getting your system documented, assist in plugging any holes that you may have, and recommend any tools or additional add-ons that you may need to make your system comply with ISO or the CMMI model. Although there are many excellent consultants out there, an organization's limited financial resources may become the deciding factor between choosing a consultant who is cheap or a consultant who is capable.

Finally, I would like to leave you with the following suggestions:

1. Remain in control of your Quality Management System and in charge of the implementation.

2. The Implementation Project–it must result in your system, your owner-ship. Remember that it is *you* who will be running the system once the consultant's input is completed.

3. If you are offered a consulting and certification or appraisal package, do not buy it, as it is not 'in line' with the requirement for independence with regard to consulting and third party certification/appraisal.

4. Do not measure the success of the implementation and the consultant's input by the size or volume of the documentation that has been developed, but rather by the involvement and commitment of your organization and the related competency that has been developed during the implementation project.

5. Ensure that all of the specific outputs of the implementation project are owned by your organization.

The discussion of this chapter centered around the make (utilizing in-house resources to chart the course for a Quality Management System and that decision must then be based on the qualifications of the quality manager within the company or the hiring of such a person) versus the buying of services through the contracting of a consultant. In either method, three factors hold true concerning the decision:

1. *Money.* What will it cost to hire a quality professional to lead the implementation and does it fit the business case and strategic objectives and goals of the company/organization? Can the consultant gain the trust and gain the confidence of both the executive management team and the employees who will need to buy-in in order to achieve a successful implementation?

2. *Time.* Regardless of the method used to implement a Quality Management System, time will be required from all levels within the organization. A seasoned and practiced consultant will adopt a coaching approach but the burden of execution rests with your implementation team, supported by the entire company/organization. Likewise, the use of an internal quality professional will also require internal resources dedicated to ensuring all activities are undertaken as an organization/company, vice one person, doing it all.

3. *Ownership.* Clearly, the more involvement and input the employees and management in your organization have in the development of the system the better the buy-in. It is hard to reject a system that you helped to cre-

ate! The clearer that you convey the reasons and objectives why your organization has endeavored to create and adopt a Quality Management System, the easier it will be for all employees to understand and support the implementation.

Chapter Four

The Realities of Getting Started

The implementation of a Quality Management System begins much like that of a roller coaster easing out from the loading platform. The roller coaster begins slowly, starting up a steep incline. The employees of your company or organization are going to feel similar as they start hearing new terms and being asked to show someone how they process a form (workflow) or how a particular activity is accomplished (sustainable processes). Are you feeling a bit antsy at hearing these terms? Now you are experiencing the ascent of the roller coaster.

In this chapter, we will leave theory and foundation behind and begin to peel back the mysteries of how to get started on your quality ride, your journey to implement a Quality Management System. Rest assured the queasiness in your stomach will subside!

Implementing a Quality Management System

Implementation of a Quality Management System affects the entire organization immediately, from the start of the implementation project. If the implementation is pursued with total dedication, it can result in a cultural transition to an atmosphere of continuous process improvement. The essential tasks as briefly described below, are proven steps to a successful implementation of a Quality Management System:

Task 1: Senior management commitment

Make it loud and make it clear! The entire executive staff, the senior managers, as well as the mid level managers must all clearly demonstrate their full support the effort. This phase cannot be lip service and it may be wise to have a very publicly displayed document signed by all managers that they are committed to this undertaking. Part of the strategy here rests with a part of human nature that compels people who sign their name publicly, to follow through on the promises that have displayed. This also serves to mediate conflicts of schedules when team members must be deployed to quality management activities.

Task 2: Conduct an initial status survey/Gap Analysis

Put simply, if you do not know where you are, then you do not know where you are going and therefore, will not know if you have ever arrived! The basic approach to a successful implementation is to rely on a proven expert, be it the quality professional you hire or appoint internally or the consultant you contract with, to determine what you have in place and what you will need to achieve a successful implementation for your Quality Management System. Much of what the analysis will show is that while your employees may not be familiar with the terms, they do have some processes and procedures they are using.

Task 3. Create a documented implementation plan/project plan

The results of the Gap Analysis serve to form the basis for the implementation/project plan. The best approach is to treat this implementation as you would any formal project, complete with a plan, schedule, budget and review points to track the progress and budget utilization.

Task 4: Establish an implementation team

Regardless of the choice of implementation, make or buy, the effort will require a team comprised from all functional areas in order to achieve success.

Task 5. Start Quality Management System awareness programs/briefings

As with any successful endeavor, knowledge and terminology are the basis for a common understanding of what is happening and being undertaken. The more exposure that employees have to the basic fundamentals of the Quality Management System, the smoother the acceptance and buy-in.

Task 6: Provide Training

There are many aspects to a Quality Management System and the entire organization must learn, understand, and implement all of them. Put another way, think back to your high school or college experiences, and remember the teacher or professor, saying, "Ladies and Gentlemen, this is testable." In order to demonstrate your organization's capabilities and understanding of the Quality Management System you implement, you will be tested!

Task 7. Establish Configuration Management/Document control

One of the key benefits of undertaking a quality ride is the ability to overcome employee frustration over "rework." Have you ever spent the time to fill out a form only to hear someone say, "That's not the correct form"? More significant is a critical task that has been completed using the wrong checklist. Having the ability to assure that your organization is using the right form, checklist, procedure etc. will more than help defray the cost of implementing your Quality Management System.

Task 8: Develop Quality Management System documentation

A system codified in documentation that has been produced by your employees is the surest way to solidify the buy-in that is needed in order to organizationally internalize the Quality Management System.

Task 9. Implementation

The journey began once the decision was made to implement a Quality Management System. The task at hand is to follow the project plan and schedule and to begin reinforcing the tenets of the Quality Management System. Meetings are held, assignments are completed, reports are generated, and peer pressure begins to surface as employees start to see the benefits of the implementation.

Suddenly, ideas are flowing, side meetings begin to happen where teams are being formed to work issues and find better ways of not only completing their individual tasks but in seeing the bigger picture that what Section A does, has an impact on Section B, C, and D.

Task 10. Internal audits

One valuable and excellent tool for helping the organization to grow is the use of internal audits. Since functional areas and individuals have now agreed to do things a set way, independent auditors from other functional areas evaluate and review for compliance to the agreed upon methods and practices. The benefit results because the auditor, coming from another functional area is suddenly exposed to many different aspects of the company or organization. As a result, horizontal communication begins to flow more freely. It is always easier to understand if you have "walked a mile, in someone else's high-heels"…uh…shoes.

Task 11. Management reviews

Essential to the success of the implementation effort is the continual feedback to management. Remember, this is an enterprise-wide endeavor. The more the management teams are involved, the easier it becomes to demonstrate the commitment that each manager signed up for on that publicly displayed document.

Task 12. Pre-assessment/Appraisal audit

You are getting close, but how close? Depending on the implementation choice, audit or appraisal teams from the accredited bodies will be contracted to come into your organization to evaluate your progress. This should be viewed as a benchmarking activity. Any impediments to a successful registration, certification, or rating will be identified during this task. Think of this as the opportunity to have a pre-test. If the implementation lead or consultant has done his/her job, this pre-assessment audit will only find minor issues for you to tweak.

Task 13. Certification/Rating

The time has come for the employees and your management team of your organization to show what they have accomplished, the knowledge they use and the processes and procedures that are in place to allow you to earn the certification or rating of the system you are implementing. It is a major undertaking and with everyone's hard work, it is a success. You are done now, right? No worries until the next required visit? Not so! The work has only just begun and the reason is based on your initial vision to all your employees. You are not buying a system, you are implementing a system designed to help you stay competitive and to grow as an organization—committed to reliable, repeatable processes and procedures and sustainable quality products and services.

Task 14: Continuous Improvement

The advantage of a Quality Management System is the ability for the organization to continually improve. Processes, procedures, and teams will remain in place to assure that continuous improvement is alive and well in your company or organization.

As far as when the right time for implementing a Quality Management System goes, in my experience the right time is as soon as possible, as early as you possibly can within your organization. The sooner that you establish these processes and build them into your everyday work, the easier it will be to meet the challenges of new business opportunities, changing work environments, and staying ahead of your competitors. A simple action such as having the capability to easily assimilate a new employee into your workforce based on having readily accessible forms and documented procedures that the employee and manager knows are current will minimize apprehension and help to confirm to your new employee that they have joined a quality organization.

From a cost perspective, it would probably be more cost efficient implementing a Quality Management System earlier on, when your employees have not institutionalized processes and work habits. The larger an organization, the bigger the turfs, and built-in resistance to change. The dreaded words of "We've always done it that way," are easily overcome when an organization is in the developmental stages of growth. The reason you want to implement as early as possible in your organization is to build quality into your processes and build the consistency, reliability and repeatability into your system early on so any new staff that comes on board understands that following these processes is a part of their job, not 'in addition' to their job. They are not going to see it as extra work! By implementing a Quality Management System early on, you maximize buy-in at the 'in-the-weeds' level. It is good practice to implement the Quality Management System being documented as the documentation is being developed, although this may be more effective in larger organizations. In smaller organizations, the Quality Management System is often implemented all at once throughout the entire organization. Where phased implementation takes place, the effectiveness of the system in selected areas can be evaluated. It would be a good idea initially to evaluate or audit areas where the chances of a positive result are high, in order to maintain the confidence of both management and staff in the merits of implementing the Quality Management System. The implementation progress should be monitored to ensure that the Quality Management System is effective and conforms to the requirements of the Quality Management System. These activities include internal quality audit, corrective action, and management review.

It is critical to get executive management to buy-in. Management will almost always tell you they are in support of the initiative, but actually getting executive management engaged in the implementation is another issue altogether.

The principal factor in choosing people to work on any team, whether it is your change control board, internal review board, your internal audit team, whatever, is in choosing people that actually *want* to be involved. I had a person once at an organization who sat in a group-training course that I had given. It was a generic training on the ISO 9000 Quality Management System. After the training, he came to me and asked if there was anything that he could do because he truly wanted to participate. He was a welder's helper and brand new to the organization. Though he was one of the lowest people on the totem pole, he had a high interest in wanting to participate and help, and showed tremendous enthusiasm. Those characteristics alone made me choose to use him on our internal audit team. He ended up being one of the best internal auditors that I had, just out of sheer enthusiasm, drive and his desire to participate.

Gap Analysis

When I arrive at a theme park, the first thing I do is try to acquire a map of the park. This way I can hunt down the rides I want to go on, and locate the snack bars and eating establishments. You actually want to do the something similar when implementing a Quality Management System. You should ascertain where you are, presently, take a 'survey of the land', and basically figure out where you are at this point in time with regard to meeting the requirements of the Quality Management System you are trying to implement. I highly recommend performing a Gap Analysis. A gap is sometimes spoken of as "the space between where we are and where we want to be." A Gap Analysis is undertaken as a means of bridging that space. A Gap Analysis, correctly performed, will tell you where you stand in relation to the standard or model that you have chosen. You can choose to contract a consulting firm to do the Gap Analysis for you or you can choose to do the Gap Analysis yourself. Once the Gap Analysis is complete, if you have chosen to do it yourself, you will probably have identified areas that were perceived as strong, but are actually lacking. You also should have identified areas that are stronger than others are. The Gap Analysis will give you an overall view of where you stand versus where you need to be. This will be of great help to you when you start to plan the implementation project. Recommended steps to be completed before conducting the Gap Analysis are:

1.   Identify one or more people to conduct the Gap Analysis; it is helpful if they have some quality system experience or audit experience. You may also want to consider having assistance from a consultant.
2.   Create or acquire a checklist for the Gap Analysis

Schedule the Gap Analysis, and communicate to all employees what is being done, and why. You will want to be able to make the employees comfortable with answering your auditor's questions. The auditor is the person conducting the Gap Analysis. It may be an audit team or one individual. A Gap Analysis can typically take approximately anywhere from 2 days to 5 days to perform. It will depend on the size of your organization, the number of auditors, the state of your current Quality Management System and the experience of your auditors.

You will want to use the completed analysis to make task lists and/or a work breakdown structure (WBS) for the implementation project plan. For each section of the Quality Management System requirements, you will want to prepare a list of items that need to be implemented, redesigned, or documented. In order to start planning, you will need to determine what your goals are for the implementation. You might want to consider the start of your implementation project as the date of the Gap Analysis.

The next several pages are intended to provide you with examples of checklists and questions you might consider using when performing your Gap Analysis.

Project Planning

The most effective means of ensuring sthat efforts of a complex nature or involving high costs in either dollars or resources is to control the effort through project management.

How does the project establish and maintain plans that define the project activities?

Questions:
1. How does your project establish the planning parameters (e.g. guidelines and constraints) for estimating its effort and cost? Is historical data used?
2. How does your project establish and maintain its plans?
3. How does your project obtain commitments to the project plan? How is this maintained?
4. Describe any processes, process documentation, co-worker/management process awareness, training and resources for project monitoring and control.
5. How does your project perform re-planning?
6. How does your project plan for the identification and analysis of risk?

CMMI Practices:
Can you find evidence of:

- Estimate the Scope of the Project

  WBS exists?
  Work packages exist in sufficient detail to estimate accurately?
  Externally acquired work products or components identified?
  Work products identified that will be reused?

- Establish Estimates of Work Product and Task Attributes

  Is technical approach identified?
  Are there methods employed to determine attributes of work products?

- Define Project Life Cycle

  Are there life cycle phases for the project?

- Determine Estimates of Effort and Cost

  Are there estimation models? Historical data?

- Establish the Budget and Schedule

  Major milestones identified?
  Do assumptions for certain schedule items exist?
  Are schedule constraints identified? Dependencies and precedence?
  Is there a schedule and a budget? Is it known when replanning is requir

- Identify Project Risks

  Are risks identified? Documented? Verified with relevant stakeholders?

- Plan for Data Management

  Is there a mechanism to archive and distribute project data?

- Plan for Project Resources

  Is there a staffing plan for the project?
  Are other project resources planned?

- Plan for Needed Knowledge and Skills
- Plan Stakeholder Involvement

  Are stakeholders identified? Are their roles identified?

- Establish the Project Plan
- Review Plans that Affect the Project
- Reconcile Work and Resource Levels
- Obtain Plan Commitment

Things to Look For:
- Project Plans
    ___QA ___ CM ___ M&A ___ Data
- Evidence of Adequate Resources and Tools
- Program Schedules and/or dependencies
- WBS

- Management training for planning
- People assigned responsibility and trained
- Risk Identification/Analysis
- Task Planning
- Coordination with stakeholders

Project Monitoring & Control

How does the project establish and maintain adequate visibility into the project's progress so that appropriate actions can be taken when there are significant deviations from the plan?

Questions:

7. How does your project monitor actual performance of the project against the plan baseline?
8. How does your project plan for and take appropriate actions when the project's performance or results deviate significantly from the plan baseline?
9. Describe any processes, process documentation, co-worker/management process awareness, training and resources for project monitoring and control.
10. How does your project monitor and record risks and risk activities?
11. Does your project revise the project plan to reflect accomplishments, progress, changes, and corrective actions as appropriate?

CMMI Practices:

Can you find evidence of:

- Monitor Project Status

  Progress against the schedule

  Cost and expended effort reports

- Monitor Commitments

- Monitor Project Risks

  Is there a risk review activity? Does it update the identified risks?

- Monitor Data Management

- Monitor Stakeholder Involvement

- Conduct Progress Reviews

  How often are reviews conducted? Who is the audience? How do we know the review occurred?

  Is the project performance evaluated at the review?

- Conduct Milestone Reviews

  How often are reviews conducted? Who is the audience? How do we know the review occurred?

  Is the project performance evaluated at the review?

- Analyze Issues

  How are issues identified and analyzed? Is corrective action taken?

- Take Corrective Actions

  How is this performed? Is the plan agreed to?

- Manage Corrective Actions

  Are corrective action plans monitored? How do you know if they can be closed?

Things to Look For:

- ❏ Revised Project Plans
- ❏ Evidence of Adequate Resources and Tools
- ❏ Status Reports
- ❏ Action Items
- ❏ People assigned responsibility and trained
- ❏ Documented program and/or milestone reviews

Supplier Agreement Management

How does the project identify, select, and manage sources of products and services used to satisfy the project's requirements?

Questions:
12. How does your project establish supplier agreements?
13. How does your project monitor and coordinate supplier status and work products?
14. How does your project ensure mutual understanding of contract scope and requirements?
15. Describe any processes, process documentation, co-worker/management process awareness, training and resources for project monitoring and control.
16. How does your project track and manage contract issues?
17. How does your project accept delivery of products or services?

CMMI Practices:
Can you find evidence of:
- Analyze Potential Sources of Products
- Incorporate requirements into the solicitation package
- Prepare cost and schedule estimates
- Review cost and schedule estimates
- Evaluate proposals
- Ensure understanding of requirements
- Establish Contractor agreements
- Monitor Selected Contractor Processes
- Evaluate Selected Work Products
- Review Non-Developmental Items
- Conduct reviews and interchanges
- Compare actual technical activities, cost and schedule to plans
- Track sustainment products
- Ensure User Evaluation of System Performance
- Take appropriate actions
- Accept delivery of products

Things to Look For:
- ❑ Source selection plans
- ❑ Results of evaluations
- ❑ Contractor progress reports and/or minutes
- ❑ Audits of Contractor processes or products
- ❑ List/status of Contract Actions
- ❑ Contractor SOW
- ❑ Contracts, task orders, ECPs
- ❑ Responsibilities assigned

Requirements Management

How does the project manage the requirements of the Project's products, and keep the projects plans and work products consistent with them?

<u>Questions:</u>
18. How are requirements managed so that they accurately reflect the program plans and work products?
19. How does your program maintain requirements traceability?
20. Describe any processes, process documentation, co-worker/management process awareness, training and resources for requirements management.
21. How does your program analyze requirements quality (completeness, clarity, etc)?
22. How does your program track work effort against requirements

<u>CMMI Practices:</u>
Can you find evidence of:
- Obtain an Understanding of Requirements
- Obtain Commitment to Requirements
- Baseline Requirements
- Analyze Requirements Change Requests
- Maintain Bidirectional Traceability of Requirements
- Identify Inconsistencies Between Program Work and Requirements

Things to Look For:

❑ Requirements Traceability Matrix	❑ People assigned responsibility and trained
❑ Requirements management tools, database	❑ Requirements Metrics
❑ Requirement issues and/or action items	❑ Evidence of Adequate Resources and Tools
❑ Results/minutes of requirements reviews	❑ Updated plans, work products, activities

Configuration Management

How does your project establish and maintain the integrity of work products using configuration identification, configuration control, configuration status accounting, and configuration audits?

Questions:
23. How does your project establish and maintain baselines of identified work products?
24. How does your project track and control changes to the work products under CM?
25. How does your project ensure the integrity of the baselines?
26. Describe any processes, process documentation, co-worker/management process awareness, training and resources for configuration management.
27. What procedures, tools and media has your project established for CM?
28. How does your project report CM status and what audits do you perform?

CMMI Practices:
Can you find evidence of:
- Identify Configuration Items
- Establish a Configuration Management System
- Create or Release Baselines
- Track Change Requests
- Control Configuration Items
- Establish Configuration Management Records
- Perform Configuration Audits

Things to Look For:
- Controlled work products
- Configuration Management Plan
- Configuration Management Status Reports
- Revision history of configured items
- CM responsibilities assigned
- Change requests and/or metrics
- CCB Minutes
- CM Tools
- Training for CM Tools and/or process

Measurement & Analysis

How does the project develop and sustain a measurement capability that supports management information needs?

Questions:

29. How does your project ensure that measurement objectives and practices are aligned with established information needs and objectives?

30. How does your project ensure that measurement results that address information needs are available?

31. Describe any processes, process documentation, co-worker/management process awareness, training and resources for measurement and analysis.

32. What data has your project collected and stored?

33. What analysis and interpretation has your project performed?

34. What training is provided to your project to support measurement collection and analysis?

CMMI Practices:

Can you find evidence of:

- Establish Measurement Objectives

  Information needs & objectives documented? Prioritized?

  Measurement needs and objectives documented? Reviewed?

  Correlation exists between measurement objectives and information needs?

- Specify Measures

  Are candidate measures identified? Are existing measures known? Are they well defined?

- Specify Data Collection and Storage Procedures

  Are there documents that specify how to collect the data for each measure? Storage archive identified?

- Specify Analysis Procedures

  Are there methods specified for analyzing the measures? Are they appropriate? Responsible person(s) identified? Communication plan exists?

- Collect Measurement Data

  Are base measures collected? Derived measures determined?

- Analyze Measurement Data

  Are the measures analyzed? Are the analyses presented to the relevant stakeholders?

- Store Data and Results

- Communicate Results

Things to Look For:

- ❏ Measurement plans and objectives
- ❏ Evidence of adequate resources and tools
- ❏ People assigned responsibility and trained
- ❏ Measures databases
- ❏ Data collection and storage procedures and/or tools
- ❏ Analysis reports, draft reports, presentations
- ❏ Collected & derived measurement data sets

Product and Process Quality Assurance

How does the project provide staff and management with objective insight into processes and associated work products?

Questions:
35. How does your project objectively evaluate processes and work products?
36. How does your project deal with non-compliance issues?
37. Describe any processes, process documentation, co-worker/management process awareness, training and resources for product and process quality assurance.
38. What data has your project collected and stored?
39. What training is provided to your project to support product and process quality assurance?

CMMI Practices:
Can you find evidence of:

- Objectively evaluate processes

  Evaluation reports, Noncompliance reports, corrective actions?
  Positive environment for reporting quality issues?
  Clearly stated criteria? What, When, How, Who?

- Objectively evaluate work products and services

  Work products selected to be evaluated? Criteria clear?

- Communicate and ensure resolution of non-compliance issues

  Corrective action taken?

- Establish records

Things to Look For:

- Quality records
- Evaluation reports
- Noncompliance reports

- Corrective actions
- Quality database

Upon completion of the gap analysis, you should be able to visually assess where you are against what the model or standard requires as illustrated in the Sample Gap Analysis Results Charts.

Sample Gap Analysis Results Charts

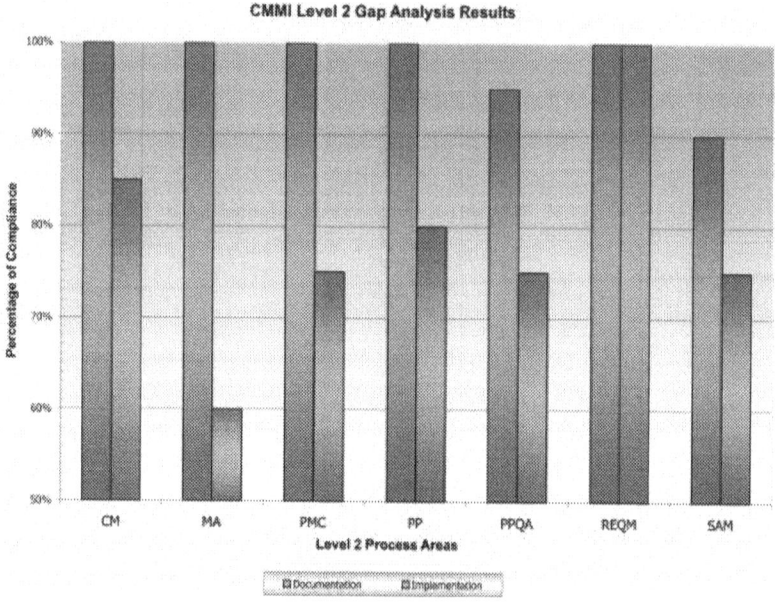

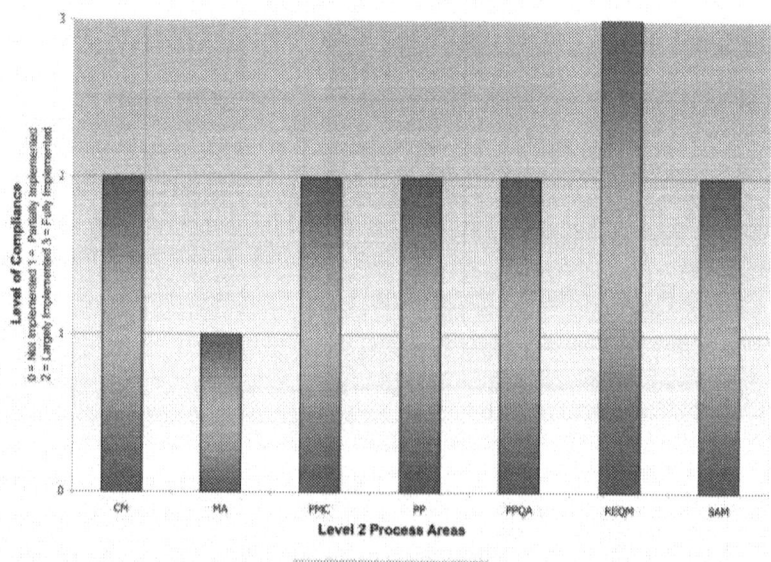

Create a Documented Implementation or Project Plan

Once your organization has obtained a clear picture of how its Quality Management System compares with the ISO 9000 standard or the CMMI model, non-conformances must be addressed with a documented implementation plan/project plan. Usually, the plan calls for identifying and describing processes that either need to be developed and/or implemented to ensure the organization's Quality Management System fully complies with the standard. The implementation plan should be thorough and specific, detailing:

1. Quality documentation to be developed
2. Objective of the system
3. Pertinent sections of the standard or model
4. Person or team responsible/POC
5. Approval required
6. Stakeholders
7. Training required
8. Resources required
9. Costs
10. Estimated completion date

These elements should be organized into a requirements document, work breakdown structure (WBS) and project schedule, to be reviewed and approved. The shorter time frame allowed for the project, the more resources the project will demand during implementation. It is important to know what your goal is because other dates will be determined by this information. Find out if there are organizational goals. Are there clients that are requesting certification or other circumstances that will determine the date? Your date may be revised later. You will use this as a target date, and as you move along to creating the WBS or task list, you will be able to determine if the date is realistic. It will depend on what you currently have in place for your Quality Management System, and how many resources you have available for the implementation project. The plan should define the responsibilities of different departments and personnel and set target dates for the completion of activities. Once approved, the project manager should control, review, and update the plan as the implementation project proceeds.

According to the Project Management Institute's *Project Management Body of Knowledge*® (PMBOK®) a project must have a distinct beginning and end. However, I have found that managing the implementation of a Quality

Management System exactly as I manage a project with the end of the project being the completed assessment, rating, or appraisal, works best for handling the myriad of activity associated with an implementation. Technically, implementing a Quality Management System could not be a project because part of the system is continuous improvement (meaning that it has no end, it is ongoing). However, I would urge organizations to treat the development and implementation of their Quality Management System as a project to give it structure, accountability, sponsorship, and buy-in.

Managing the implementation of your Quality Management System as a project will assist you in developing the scope of the work, defining tasks, estimating resources, determining timeframes, noting risks, and gaining stakeholder buy-in. You want to be sure to factor in time for risks, which may include change in priorities, no money, no resources, low buy-in on new processes, etc. (See Figure 1). Risk management is a continuous, forward-looking process that addresses potential problems that could endanger achievement of product/project goals. A continuous risk management approach effectively anticipates and mitigates the risks that impact your implementation project.

You also want to assemble any teams that are necessary and define the teams' roles. Those teams can include a change control board, an internal audit team, or teams of that nature. Also, target a date for introductory training for all employees. You will want your employees to be aware of the project, what will need to be done, who will be involved, and why you are implementing a Quality Management System.

Get Everyone in the Organization Speaking the Same Language

It is fairly common for employees of organizations to have varying degrees of exposure to different types of Quality Management Systems. This being the case, not everyone will be "speaking the same language". One method for ensuring everyone is speaking the same language is to develop and deploy a standard Glossary of Terms for your organization that includes definitions and acronyms. Understanding the function of different types of documents within your organization may be muddled or unclear because there may be many people in your organization that come from various backgrounds with diverse degrees of experiences pertaining to Quality Management Systems. When looking at the pyramid below, you can see that the top of the pyramid shows the 'policy' document. The next tier in the pyramid are the documents that describe 'who, what, why, where, when' and support the policy document(s). The third tier of documents in the pyramid describe how specific activities are performed and support the 'who, what where, when, and why' documents. Finally, the last tier of documents in the pyramid are documents that provide evidence of an activity being performed and they support the 'how' documents.

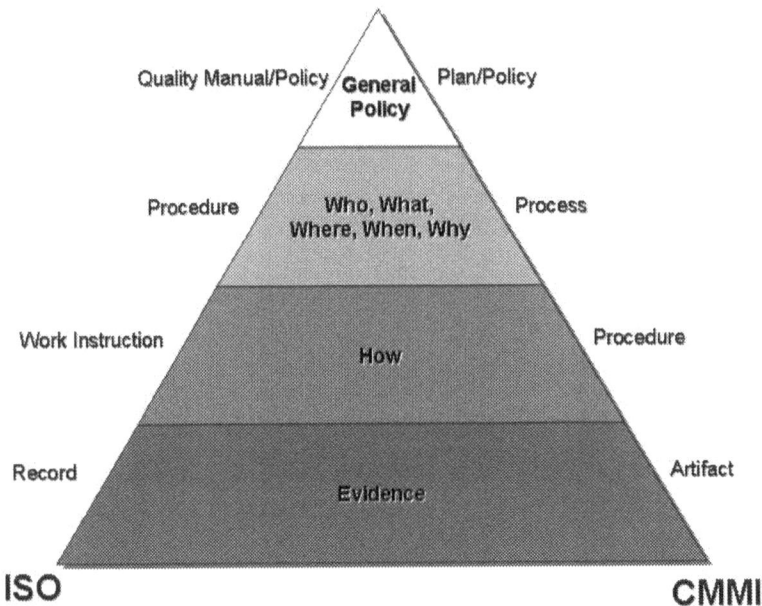

It is most important during an implementation that all employees understand the function of each type of document, whatever you choose to call them.

It doesn't matter what you call the document.

What matters is... what the document does and what other documents it supports.

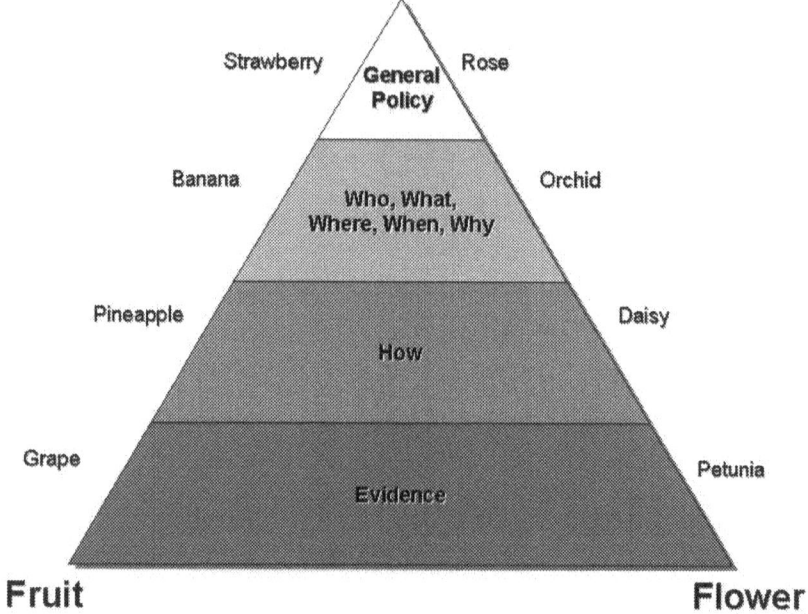

Document Control/Change Control

You want to target the development or introduction of the critical foundational processes first. As a rule, I set up document control and/or change control first. This way, there is an established mechanism for handling all of the new or revised processes and procedures as they are being developed. Creating the document control and/or change control system first has always been most effective for me in the long run. When you are developing your document control and change control systems, you may find that much of your staff will have a hard time only using those approved processes or procedures. They may say things like "Well, that procedure isn't how we really do it", or they will use outdated or unapproved procedures that reside on someone's hard drive. That is a part of the cultural change. Your documents must reflect what is currently being done, not the way you want things done in a perfect world. Employee involvement is critical to the success of an implementation project. There may be times when it seems easier to do it yourself, but you will benefit ultimately by delegating. Stick to the plan of delegating the responsibility for writing the processes and procedures to those who are responsible for actually doing the work. The documents will be developed better, building on the day-to-day experiences and knowledge of the people working with them. You will have buy-in from process and procedure owners. When you start using the new processes and procedures, you will be able to avoid the situation of rolling out the documents just to hear that they will not work. This is a case of "Don't just do it." Involve others!

Your documents must go through an approval process then the documents must be placed in a repository that has access controls so that not just anyone can make changes but everyone has access to view the documents. I would recommend a web-based collaborative work environment such as SharePoint or something that is similar. So whether you choose to use a paper system or an electronic system, all of your approved processes, procedures, and forms must be available for use by all employees. Once the necessary Quality Management System documentation has been generated, a documented system must be created to control it. Control is simply a means of managing the creation, approval, distribution, revision, storage, and disposal of the various types of documentation. Document control systems should be as simple and as easy to operate and navigate as possible—sufficient to meet Quality Management System requirements and that is all. Document control should include:

- Approval for adequacy by authorized person(s) or entities before issue,
- Review, updating and re-approval of documents by authorized person(s) or entities,
- Identification of changes and of the revision status of documents,
- Availability of relevant versions of documents,
- Identification and control of documents of external origin, and
- Prevention of unintended use of obsolete documents.

The tenet of document control is that employees should have access to the documentation and records needed to fulfill their job responsibilities.

A further objective that I have in the beginning when I work with an organization to implement a Quality Management System is to gather all their existing documentation. Some, maybe even all of the documentation gathered may be of use whether it is forms, procedures, work instructions, manuals, or just about anything. You never know what prize you may find that's been sitting on someone's hard drive or shelf!

Meeting Minutes

Another key item that you might want to consider implementing as soon as possible would be the taking very concise meeting minutes. Particularly when you are implementing CMMI, meeting minutes can prove to be extremely beneficial in an appraisal. Your meeting minutes can be evidence of consensus and your meeting minutes can show that action items were identified and addressed and that there has been communication through the ranks, particularly when you take meeting minutes at a more senior level. Meeting minutes can reflect that there has been communication with each other and among functional areas. Taking meeting minutes and storing them as artifacts or records can be very advantageous.

Data Collection

Many organizations are unaware that they are actually already doing much of what the Quality Management System calls for in connection with ISO or CMMI requirements. In some cases, functional areas within an organization are already collecting data. They may not be generating metrics from the data or analyzing those metrics but they are at least collecting the data. That is where you would want to focus, or have your quality department or personnel go to gather that data, create and analyze the metrics, and then forward those analyses to management for action. Functional areas are sometimes surprised to find out that they are in effect doing many tasks that a Quality Management System requires. Your job will be to wrap your arms around those processes and procedures that are already being done, fine tune them and make them consistent, reliable and repeatable.

Corrective and Preventive Action

Other functions that I normally choose to implement right away are corrective action with root cause analysis, and preventive action. Root cause analysis is particularly important for those of you in service industries because if you wait to collect data for an extended amount of time before you actually do causal analysis and resolution (or root cause analysis), you may wind up losing a customer. Predictably, when an issue happens you want to find the root cause then correct it as soon as possible to prevent recurrence. So causal analysis and resolution, root cause analysis, or whatever you choose to call it depending on the Quality Management System that you are following, is a good idea to implement right away predominantly in manufacturing and services industries. Several books are available that detail the basics of root cause analysis, and there are several methods and/or tools that you can use for performing root cause analysis.

The Organization Chart

Why would you need an organization chart? An organization chart details the support structure for all of your individual processes, and it also gives roles and responsibilities required for each of the particular blocks on the org chart. A benefit might be that the organization chart will allow your customers to see the support structure for the products or services that they are buying from you. Another benefit can be that the clearly defined roles and responsibilities give a clear understanding of the job for a person who is new, and that the documentation of the roles and responsibilities does not leave anything to interpretation that might vary from person to person within your organization. Clearly, a detail as small as establishing an organization chart can bring a value to your system.

Know Your Audience!

Usually during the first month, I try to acclimate myself with the way the organization is functioning, working beside people, getting to know what they do, who they are and how they work, and how the different departments work together to get a real feel for the organization and gain a better understanding of how things operate within that organization. This is critical when implementing a Quality Management System because you truly have to know the organization's culture and have a good understanding of it. That is the only way that you are going to be able to plan for and predict the cultural changes that will inevitably happen.

In the business world, the products and services that your customers are getting from you are not just the physical services that you provide, they are every contact point that the customer touches. That includes marketing, accounting, management beliefs or organizational vision-mission, goals, objectives, human resources, recruiting, etc. This means that everything that your organization does is the product. The business is the product that the customer is purchasing and it is the product the customer demands consistency from every time, everyday. Therefore, the real issue becomes what your management is doing to produce the consistent solution that delivers a consistent benefit to a clearly defined set of customers. That being the case, the first thing to do is implement a Quality Management System. Then you have instituted a baseline. Once your processes are in place and you have established consistency, you can take steps to improve your processes, thus insuring that your customers are getting the best possible product and/or service that you can provide for them.

Starting With A Blank Page–Don't!

When attempting to document your Quality Management System and document the processes and procedures that you currently use for the activities that you do, <u>do not</u> hand anyone a blank page and expect them to be able to define their processes and procedures. More often than not, you will find yourself waiting a long time for the document and if and when you finally get something, it typically will not be what you expected. Roll your sleeves up and give them a hand! For example, during the development and implementation of my first Quality Management System, I realized as I reviewed the standard that I did not have first-hand knowledge of the jobs that were being performed on the manufacturing floor, and I needed to get that knowledge so that these procedures could be documented. Now on average, it is very difficult to ask a welder to write down what they are doing and why they are doing it, how they are doing it, when and where. So I rolled my sleeves up, put on my hard hat, and steel toed shoes, walked out on the manufacturing floor and started interviewing all of the different workers, taking a surplus of notes and in some cases, flowcharting the workflow as it moved, and the product as it moved from one area to another. I ended up with work instructions and procedures, which once in draft form, I was able to give to the work center supervisors for mark up. I was able to map processes based on most of the interviews also.

Realizing that you have a Quality Management System in place does not necessarily mean that your product or service is good. You can consistently make a bad product or service and still have a Quality Management System in place, but eventually you will go out of business. Conversely, you can consistently make a good product and/or service, making your customers happy, and as a result, you will grow your business. A Quality Management System developed, implemented, and maintained correctly can ensure that you are doing what you are doing consistently and reliably and that it is repeatable. That means that if you are not improving your processes, you may be doing things incorrectly or not as good as they could be done consistently. When an organization views a Quality Management System as a process to more effectively manage its business operations, the benefits can be considerable, the cost of poor quality can be reduced, management-employee skills can be significantly enhanced, continuous process improvement can insure lasting results, and you can end up with a framework to manage your organization more effectively. Through establishing objectives, benchmarking practices and a structure for employee input, measurable effectiveness, and efficiency can be achieved.

Work Smart—Not Hard: Acquiring or Developing Tools

In my opinion, it is always best to work smart not hard! This is why we are going to talk about acquiring or developing tools. In the technological society that we live in now, it is much easier to get away from hard copy and go electronic. However, tools can be very expensive. The best thing that you can do is evaluate your needs and then evaluate the custom tools that are available as well as the commercial off-the-shelf (COTS) tools that are available. You may be able to find the tool that would accommodate your needs that may be cost effective. On the other hand, it might not be cost effective and you may want to consider developing something in-house. Alternatively, you may already have something in-house that you could tweak.

In the case of the current Quality Management System that I developed, we use the SharePoint portal (which is a Microsoft COTS product) as our repository and collaborative work environment. We also have custom tools that were developed in-house in a.NET framework that handle many of our quality needs such as corrective action, change control, supplier quality, non-conformance reports, receiving inspection, etc. and that database has been critical in moving forward with process improvement. We also have another in-house tool for project management, which serves as both a repository and database—collecting issues, risks with a risk log, and project input reports. When it comes to tools, you categorically want to define your needs and target the areas that would benefit from having a tool in place.

In conclusion, in this chapter we identified that the implementation of a Quality Management System affects the entire organization. We also looked at the fourteen essential tasks to a successful implementation of a Quality Management System. As discussed, involvement of senior management has to be visibly demonstrated throughout the duration of the implementation, if not, the implementation will suffer the same quick death as other management endeavors that have been killed off by the infamous resistance to change.

Figure 1. Example Project Schedule

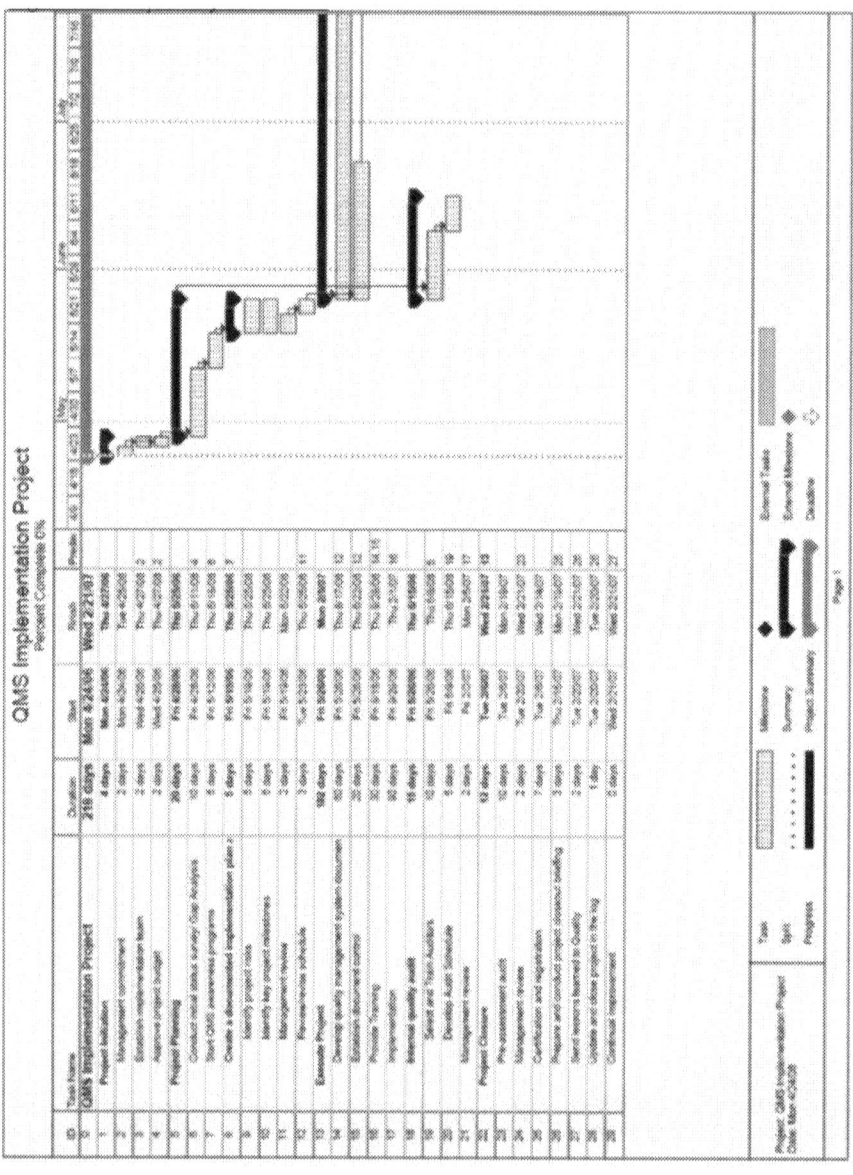

Chapter Five

Cultural Change

This chapter addresses the cultural changes that must occur to ensure that all your employees come to embrace, live, and breathe quality. Do not be afraid, shaking up the culture for the purpose of improving the organization is not a bad thing, as long as the reasons for the change are clearly communicated to every employee in the organization. There was a story about President Lyndon Johnson and an encounter with a janitor at NASA. When President Johnson asked the janitor, who was busily mopping a floor, what he was doing. The janitor replied, "I'm putting a man on the moon." This is an example of a person who understands the focus and commitment to the organization.

In order to get your people on the roller coaster ride, senior management should get in the roller coaster car first! This will show commitment to the others taking the ride and make the commitment visible. Similarly, senior management must demonstrate a commitment and determination to implement a Quality Management System within your organization. Without senior management commitment, no quality initiative can succeed. Senior management must be convinced that the registration, certification, or rating will enable the organization to demonstrate to its customers a visible commitment to quality. They should realize that a Quality Management System would provide overall business efficiency by the elimination of wasteful duplication and rework.

Senior management should provide evidence of its commitment to the development and implementation of the Quality Management System and continuously improve its effectiveness by communicating to the organization the importance of meeting internal and external customer requirements, as well as statutory and regulatory requirements, and ensuring that quality objectives are established at all levels and functions. Senior management should also ensure the availability of resources required for the development and implementation of the Quality Management System and should regularly conduct management reviews. Senior management should also consider actions such as leading the organization by example, participating in improvement projects, and creating an environment that encourages the involvement of all people.

This type of senior management commitment may be driven by direct marketplace pressure, the requirements of crucial customers, indirect marketplace pressure, increased quality levels of visibility among competitors, growth ambitions, a desire to exploit market opportunities, or a personal belief in the value of quality as a goal and Quality Management Systems as a means of reaching that goal.

Senior management should identify the goals to be achieved through the Quality Management System. Examples of some of those goals may be for the organization to be more efficient and profitable, or to produce products and/or services that consistently meet or exceed customers' needs and expectations, to achieve better customer satisfaction, increase the organization's market share, improve communications and morale within the organization, reduce costs and liabilities, or increase confidence in the system.

Frequently senior management in an organization will give a person within that organization a directive to implement a Quality Management System, and the executives may have little or no knowledge of the standard or model to be used. This could result in a lack of support when senior management discovers that the person they appointed cannot implement the Quality Management System alone and in a vacuum. Without the correct authority or empowerment sanctioned by senior management, any efforts to manage a cultural change are inevitably doomed. Any organization that pursues developing and implementing a Quality Management System without being fully committed to the process has little chance of success in achieving the long-term goals. Worse, without genuinely committing to the process, they will waste valuable resources on a futile quest.

When asked about the nature of biggest cultural change within his company since implementation began, Richard Bechtold said, "Mostly it has been a function of becoming highly systematic in numerous technical, managerial, and support areas. There is still plenty of room for creativity, but there are now numerous areas where systems are in place to help ensure sustained efficiency and effectiveness."

Some key indicators that management is committed to the development and implementation of a Quality Management System can be the eagerness to develop, write, implement, train on, and review their own procedures and processes; also providing adequate staffing and resources. Another key indicator that senior management is committed might be senior management having scheduled meetings or briefings with regard to the status of the development and implementation process and how that is going. If senior management is regularly scheduling an all hands meeting to brief the organization, you know that they are being involved, they know what is going on, want everybody else to know what is going on, and that they are supporting it.

A key indicator that senior management is <u>not</u> committed to development and implementation of a Quality Management System is when they procrastinate, or insist that you revise your implementation schedule, or find ways to circumvent or extend deadlines. This clearly indicates that the implementation is not a priority to senior management and sends that message out very clearly. Another key indicator that senior management may not be committed is by the lack of support from their subordinates or their subordinates are completely unaware of what they are supposed to be doing. There is no leadership from above. There is no communication from above. Not responding quickly to issues or roadblocks that may stifle the process can be a clear indication of lack of commitment. That is another version of "If I ignore it, maybe it will just go away."

Implementing a Quality Management System involves a radical change in attitudes. The defense of the status quo, and resistance to innovation, cannot be treated as normal management behavior. A fear of reprisals for reporting or identifying problems or issues has to be replaced by congratulating people for identifying opportunities for improvement. The hoarding of good ideas within functional areas needs to become a thing of the past as people share their knowledge and experience in the pursuit of greater organizational success. Richard Bechtold points out,

> Typically, one of the largest cultural changes I see in client organizations is significant improvements in accountability. People have a

much better sense of who is responsible for what. Another significant change is often dramatically improved visibility and communication. People have a much better overall awareness of what is happing around them, and how their actions or inactions impact others.

Resistance to Change

Another issue with cultural change is going to be "resistance from the troops". In almost every case where I have implemented a Quality Management System, the general consensus is "this is going to be more work for me". You will hear comments and excuses, like "I don't have the time," "You haven't given me enough direction." In many cases people will ignore it, thinking that, "oh well, this is just another management grand idea, and if we ignore it long enough it will go away" and believe it or not in some cases, people may even pretend that they don't understand what you're trying to do as a method of dodging. People will not want to get in on the project unless they know what it means to them and to their job. Explain why the Quality Management System is important to the organization, explain how it will make their job easier, and explain how their job will be different *and* how it will be the same. Understand that employees may feel threatened. You may hear statements or questions like, "If I document every-thing I do, will I still have value", or "What is this corrective action? It sounds like going to the principals office", or "Someone is going to audit my performance?" Your job is to remove the perceived threat. Involve your employees in the devel-opment process, and train your staff on corrective action and internal audits emphasizing the focus on improving processes.

When I was in the Navy, one of my instructors in my A school said something that genuinely stuck in my mind, partly because he would tap on my welding shield with a rod while he was saying it, and partly because he said it every time I talked to him. He said, "Repetition is the key to learning." When you're imple-menting cultural change, particularly with regard to implementing a Quality Management System, you want to boil it down in its simplest terms and con-stantly repeat what you truly want the masses to understand, the basics.

People naturally fear change. You may hear things like, "Well, we've been doing it this way for the last 20 years." That does not necessarily mean that they have been doing it correctly for the last 20 years or that the way that they have been doing it works for the organization today. One of my favorite discussions on the topic of doing something for 20 years is by Tom Peters, who equates someone saying that they have 20 years experience as possibly having one experience repeated 20 times! Unfortunately, that is all a part of cultural change. People are resistant to change, not to mention resistant to new technology. If you, in your developing and implementing of a Quality Management System, introduce new tools that automate tasks or that establish workflow, and people are used to doing these things manually, they will fight it. The key there is persistence. Frequently during the phases of implementation, people will fight, fight, fight it, and finally when they start using a new automated system, months later they will not be able to recall what they did before you implemented the system. That is just a natural course, and you must remain persistent. Typical complaints that you will hear—"Well, it takes away from my daily work," "I have higher priorities," "Why do we need our process put down on paper?" "I don't think that anyone needs to know how my department does what we do," "I don't need to develop a process because it's built into my system," "Wouldn't it better if we did it this way instead of a new way?"

Characteristically you will notice that people will rearrange their schedules in order to avoid development and implementation tasks so that they do not have time. It is just another way of dodging things. What you need to remember as far as cultural change goes is that people will give you many different excuses. You need to remember that they are, in fact, <u>excuses</u>. There is no viable reason why people cannot perform their duties consistently the same way every time and have their processes documented.

Persistence and accountability play a huge part in implementing a Quality Management System, and really digging into that cultural change. You need to start setting deadlines and assigning those resources for every task. You will get resistance. You will run into people that complain about it with the same over-used excuse, "I don't have enough time." The way that I found to get around that excuse is to simply explain to them, "Well, why don't we both stay after for an extra half an hour, and I will help you through this?" Most people respond better to deadlines and perceived new tasks if you are willing to sit with them and walk them through it. My Uncle Dominic always said, "If you don't want someone in your face, don't give them a reason to be there." Basically, you need to let the people in your organization know that this is not going away, and if they do not want you at their doorstep all the time, they are going to need to do whatever it takes to make sure that you are not parked there. It is a pay me now or pay me later situation and whether it be now or later, you will be paid! Now this is where the persistence comes in. You cannot back down. You cannot give up. Dig your heels in. You are going to have to be persistent. It is tiresome but necessary and effective. You are also going to have to have a thick skin because while the implementation is going on and the cultural change continues, there will be people that will fight back, for lack of a better term, by whatever means necessary. Either they will try to pick apart your work, or they may try to pick you apart as a person. There are many different tactics for doing this. That is an element of the resistance.

The solution is to push forward regardless of whether a process or system is perfect or not. You cannot improve on a process unless you have a process established to improve upon. One of the risks that you may encounter during an implementation is trying to gain consensus from everyone. This is a resistance tactic that has been used over and over again. People may 'blow holes' in something repeatedly to inhibit or prolong implementation. The solution to this issue is to get your document to where it is good enough and it works—it does not have to be perfect—then deploy your process. You can improve upon it later. At least then, you are in the game, and you are also sending a message that you are not going to let the naysayers or pessimists get in the way of moving forward.

Unless you institutionalize the right attitude by supporting it with policies, procedures, records, technologies, resources, and structures, you will never achieve the standards of quality that other organizations seem to be able to achieve. Unless you establish a quality attitude by creating a quality system, you will never achieve a world-class standard of quality. When the question of what was the nature of the biggest cultural change within your organization since implementation began was posed, Kristine Titzer emphasized the following: "More work–paperwork and cross-functional coordination. There is no getting around the fact that a good Quality Management System means additional work. However, there is also no getting around the fact that a good Quality Management System helped achieve an average customer satisfaction rating of 4.5 or higher on a 5.0 scale across projects. The high quality outputs led to job satisfaction and lower than normal turnover. The organization and staff were very proud of their achievements, though they may have grumbled a bit about the extra work"

Implementing a Quality Management System is not for the faint of heart. There will be people who will challenge you regularly. There will be people who will see you walking down the hall, turn around, and run the other way. It is not personal; it is business. But unfortunately in the workplace you're dealing with so many different types of personalities and cultures that not everybody is going to understand that it's not personal and they may feel as if you are doing this to them personally or take it as a personal affront. That is not the case. You need to remember, "it's not personal, it's business" when you are implementing a Quality Management System, and you need be tenacious and have a "thick skin".

In closing, implementing a Quality Management System involves a radical change in attitudes. The defense of the status quo, and resistance to innovation, cannot be treated as normal management behavior. Unless you institutionalize the right attitude and support it with policies, procedures, records, tools, technologies, resources, and structures, you may never achieve the standards of quality that other organizations seem to be able to achieve.

Chapter Six

The Implementation Roller Coaster Ride

You will notice in the Phases of the Quality Ride graphic (Figure 2) that there are typically four phases of the implementation roller coaster ride.

In phase one, the foundation for the implementation is being set. You are just getting started. You have assessed your strengths and weaknesses and have begun to introduce new concepts, terms, and practices that begin to focus the organization on the journey. You can think of this as the process of purchasing the ticket and lining up for the roller coaster ride. The wait for the ride to begin seems endless but time does move forward and you can feel the restlessness of the crowd as their turn for a ride comes closer. When you are getting started in development and implementation, it is much like going up that first hill of a roller coaster. You are sitting in the roller coaster car, and the ride is scarcely beginning. The anticipation is building, and any action seems to be taking forever.

In phase two, as you are developing and implementing your standard processes and procedures, things seem to drag on forever, and it seemingly takes an interminable amount of time to get up that first hill of the roller coaster ride. It is important during the implementation to target the weak areas of your organization, which you have identified through your gap analysis. What you will not be able to readily identify is where the pockets of resistance to change will occur.

You have to be prepared to rapidly address the reasons for the initial resistance and to move quickly to overcome the concerns and doubts that will inevitably be voiced. Each implementation that I undertake has shown me that the pockets of resistance cannot be predicated to a specific organizational area or function, it depends on the maturity of the organization, the past experience of the employees and sometimes it comes down to a simple breakdown in communication, where a group of people have not gotten the proper information regarding the implementation. In addition, to respond to the concerns of individuals and address the gaps for implementation, you will have the opportunity to identify and capture some quick wins, what I like to call going after the "low hanging fruit". This might be something as simple as recognizing a section or division that has written processes or prescribed procedures that everyone follows. Small, quick successes build buy-in, and you want to really focus on gaining those small, quick successes during phase two.

Figure 2. Phases of the Quality Ride

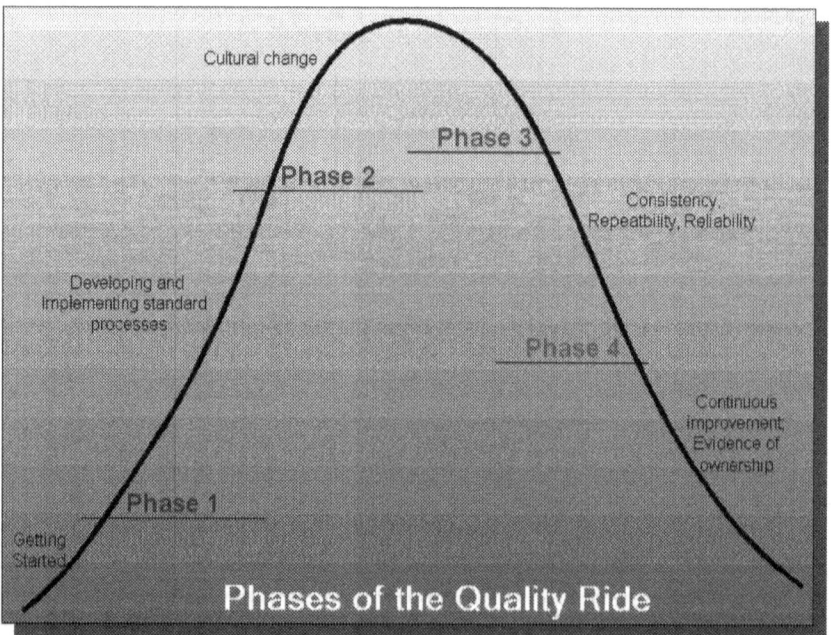

As you are ending phase two and entering phase three, you are going to notice the cultural change or shift in the focus of the employees and company as a whole. If you look at the phases of the quality ride on the graphic, you will see the cultural changes at the top, at that crest of the hill, when you are just getting to the top of that ride, and you are looking down, and your anxiety will have reached its peak. When you start getting into phase three, that is when most of the cultural change has already occurred, and you start noticing that consistency, repeatability, and reliability in your processes are beginning to emerge, and that most of your cultural change has truly permeated your organization. This also results in a faster pace and a gain of momentum. Your staff will start to pick things up more quickly. You will notice a change in the attitudes of your employees, and what your employees embrace. You will hear people talk about the Quality Management System, and they will start holding each other accountable for adhering to your established processes. You will find that many of the small wins that you have had and small successes that you have experienced during the development and implementation will have taken hold, and people will be helping each other. Moreover, it is similar to a domino effect throughout the organization as you are going through phase three.

Then finally, when you begin to approach phase four, you will notice that the "troops" will start noticing ways to improve the processes that they helped create. That is when you are getting close to the end of the ride, it seems that suddenly everyone has truly embraced the Quality Management System, and people start trying to find ways to improve upon what has been implemented. That is when you know you have successfully implemented the Quality Management System. So particularly in phase three and phase four, changes happen very quickly. Why? Because you have gained momentum and had frequent small successes—you are swooping down that hill! The employees have embraced the change and wrapped their arms around what has become their system.

We have looked at the four phases when implementing a Quality Management System. We have examined phase one where concern, confusion, and uncertainty are the norm. The employees are looking at the executives to see if there is a true commitment to this effort. We next move into phase two where the standards and processes begin to take shape and you are working on your weaknesses identified in the gap analysis, and beginning to look for and celebrate small wins. You progress now into phase three where the true shift or change in your culture begins to emerge and become visible. The employees are beginning to see and better yet, understand what the Quality Management System can do and what it means to them. Finally, we examined phase four where true employee ownership of the implementation takes hold.

We will next discuss what battles have to be fought, what ground needs to be given up in order to win the war, and why it is important to know the difference.

Chapter Seven

Choosing Your Battles

To be successful in implementing a Quality Management System, you need to recognize that not all employees will initially embrace the change, and that in some instances outright resistance to the staff responsible for the implementation will happen. How these situations are handled will certainly affect the ability to effectively implement a Quality Management System.

It is important to realize when you are implementing a Quality Management System that there are going to be many little battles and skirmishes along the way. Now obviously you cannot fight all of them, and it is important to realize that you do not necessarily want to. What constitutes a battle is something you have to identify for yourself. Does the fact that one person refusing to follow pre-scribed procedures create World War III? Well it depends on the critical nature or function of those procedures. Likewise, how do you handle a division chief who constantly misses deadlines? You want to engage in those battles that are actually going to yield you your end-result or are absolutely necessary for you to achieve that end-result. In this case, that means the effective implementation of your Quality Management System, on time and within budget. If it is something that you can work around somehow, some way, you might want to reconsider whether it is, in actuality, necessary for you to engage in that particular battle. You are going to have a lot of them, so you need to be selective about which battles you choose to fight.

For example, during one implementation, all of the quality team met with a functional area to discuss establishing data collection and generating metrics that would be meaningful for them. What the functional area opted for measuring and what they probably should be measuring were two entirely different things. The metric that the quality team ended up generating for that particular area really did not do much for them in the way of providing them the information they actually required for ensuring the effectiveness of their processes. Now for the purposes of implementing a Quality Management System, they were measuring something…that is accurate, and that is what they needed to do. However, knowing that it was not particularly meaningful for them was not a battle that I chose to fight at that time. I wanted to get them engaged first, and then improve upon it later. As an aside, after the implementation and the processes and understanding on the effectiveness of meaningful metrics tracking took hold, the functional area requested a change to their metrics to better serve their requirements. That is just one example of how you may want to choose your battles wisely. At least if you make some progress it is better than fighting a losing battle and then getting nothing at all.

When defining your implementation project, it is important to establish the difference between the necessary or required components and deliverables and those that are desirable but not absolutely necessary. One way to do this can be to define your needs versus your wants. This yields a short list of those things that must be part of your implementation project as opposed to a long list of all the things that could be part of the project. Some 'wants' are more important than others but none of them are absolutely necessary for success. Rank the list of wants in order of importance with the most important being at the top of the list and the others in descending order of importance down to the level of, "That would be nice but it's not critical if we can't do it."

Perspective

Frequently when you are implementing a Quality Management System and you hear your staff complain that you are giving them extra work, that is because they are looking at it from the perspective of they never had to do that before. So now, anything new, even though it is for the betterment of the company or for the efficiency or ease of their job, is going to be perceived as being extra work. Does that mean that it is correct? Not necessarily. To handle the resistance to change and the "excuse" factor, as I call it, I make sure to explain the value in the changes being put in place. For example, as employees begin to see the efficiency in having a centralized location for current forms or established processes for filing and retrieving data, they begin to understand that they work they do initially translates into a more efficient means of doing their work, which translates into less work in the end.

Here is the different perspective for you. If you are viewing this from the standpoint of your customers, your customers are already paying for quality that is inherent to the service or product that you provide. Your customers are naturally assuming that when they buy a product or service from you, that you have already built quality into your processes prior to delivering that product or service. Which means from that perspective, if you do not have a quality built in to your system, you have not been providing the customer what they have been paying for all along, which means you have been affording a reason for your customers to go elsewhere. So implementing these quality processes and procedures will help your employees do their jobs consistently and effectively and will help provide you with a competitive advantage in serving your customer base.

In closing, you have been given some things to consider as you face the choice of what battles to fight and which to choose to defer, ignore, or work around. Time and momentum are paramount to a successful implementation. Keeping the end objective of a successful implementation will help maintain a perspective on the issues you will confront.

Chapter Eight

Common Pitfalls and How to Avoid Them

Some common pitfalls are expecting too much (i.e. a Quality Management System will take care of my personnel, financial, and configuration management or document control problems), and not factoring in human nature, not taking into account for organizational or cultural change, or thinking that implementing the Quality Management System is going to fix your organizational or cultural change issues. It may or may not. Another pitfall is waiting to deploy until its perfect–commonly referred to as "analysis paralysis". As you are developing procedures and processes, if you wait until you think it is absolutely perfect to deploy it, you will probably be waiting a very long time. Waiting to gain unanimous consensus is another pitfall that feeds right into waiting to deploy until it is perfect.

The Quality Management System Will Fix All Our Problems

Establishing a Quality Management System will not necessarily fix all of your problems. However, it will help you to pinpoint and identify those areas where your problems do exist so that you can then take action to fix those problems. For instance, if you are expecting that your Quality Management System will take care of your personnel issues, what you will find is through implementing the Quality Management System, the dead weight will definitely rise to the surface and make itself known. However, the Quality Management System will not make employees do their job correctly, consistently or effectively. That is something that you are going to have to do.

With regard to financial issues, a Quality Management System, when implemented properly, will help you identify those areas where you may be unnecessarily spending profit money. A cost of quality analysis (COQ) can assist with that. Regarding issues pertaining to configuration management or document control problems, implementing a Quality Management System will help you identify those areas of weakness within those particular systems, but it will not necessarily fix those issues. If you have problems with document control, you may want to look into developing more high-end system in-house, maybe getting a canned software program. But, realistically, implementing a Quality Management System will not solve all your problems. It will help you *identify* those issues and narrow them down, but it will not solve all your problems.

One Man Show

Frequently when you are getting started on implementing a Quality Management System, senior management may believe that they can bring one person in, assign one person, or have a consulting company come in and the implementation will be taken care of. The flaw in that thought process is that management does not understand that they cannot just hire or appoint one full-time person to come in, and that person is going to be able to do everything for them. It takes an entire organizational effort to make a successful implementation happen with someone obviously in a lead role.

Human Nature

Many organizations, when embarking on implementing a Quality Management System, do not truly factor in human nature when they are planning for a cultural change within the organization. Everyone wants to think that their organization is full of people that actually want to embrace change, and that want the best for the organization. Nevertheless, human nature dictates that people are inherently afraid of change. They have a fear of the unknown. You would be surprised at what areas and what people will really put up resistance. Probably the single most debilitating force behind resistance and procrastination is not knowing where to start. Remember, the priority is not to decide where to start, but simply doing something, to act.

Perfection

Another pitfall that you may run into–and more than likely you will—is waiting to deploy until it is perfect or waiting to gain unanimous consensus. I worked at an organization once where, before a new process was approved for deployment and implementation, it was decided by management that everyone had to agree and approve the process. That caused problems because there were a few people on the approval board that were resistant to change, and as a result, every time the process came up for review, they would argue little bits and pieces into the ground so that the process never got implemented or deployed. Finally, we were able to show management that their edict of unanimous consensus was affecting the overall implementation of the Quality Management System. It also sets an inappropriate example for the rest of the organization, sending the message that if you just resist, ignore, or fight something to death, nothing will get done. You cannot allow that to happen!

Waiting Too Long To Implement

Time can become a severe limitation for a small business. Implementation of a Quality Management System and ultimately, registration or appraisal of that system, may take anywhere from nine to eighteen months, depending upon a variety of factors, including resources, management commitment, and employee buy-in. The organization may be pressured by customers to implement the Quality Management System within a certain time frame or potentially lose their business. It behooves small organizations to become aware of external pressures within their industry and become proactive rather than ending up behind the eight ball.

Not Understanding the Requirements for Implementing

In well-managed organizations, a Quality Management System is what they do every day. Organizations who struggle with Quality Management System implementations are generally those who look for shortcuts to the "plaque on the wall in reception" that allows their business to continue. They generally send their Quality department people on a weeklong course and expect them to understand the intricacies of the Quality Management System. When they return from the course, they are expected to implement and get certified within six months of the course. This is a pitfall, insufficient training, and understanding of the requirements of the Quality Management System.

You should agree on a practical period of time to allow for Quality Management System development and implementation, bearing in mind that it will take at least three to nine months to build the system and train all staff, another three or more months to produce the necessary records to show the system is working, and then another three or more months to complete the certification or appraisal process and receive the certificate or rating. Organizations have done it in less time, but the pressure on the implementation team definitely shows!

Skipping a Gap Analysis

Another common pitfall is not conducting an initial review or Gap Analysis. The Gap Analysis basically establishes where you are with respect to the requirements of the Quality Management System. It also identifies how you do things and what your organizational culture or work style is. Most organizations address some of the requirements in their every day operations, but do not realize that what they are doing may meet many of the standard's requirements because the "labels" are different. Poor consultants will skip this stage by offering the client an off-the-shelf solution. So the unsuspecting client falls for the easy implementation option (from the consultants point of view), but ends up with a system that is purely an add-on to his or her existing methods. This increases everyone's work and adds no value to day-to-day operations and management. So the message is…tailor the Quality Management System to fit what you do, and not tailor what you do to fit the system.

Lack of Staff Training

Insufficient staff training is an area of concern regarding cost, how much training? How often? What materials? You should focus on what your staff needs to know to do their jobs and comply with the Quality Management System requirements, so that you do not waste a lot of time showing all the "troops" the structure and content within the Quality Management System, when all they really might need to know is how to do a change request! Make all employees aware of upcoming appraisals or audits and let them know what to expect. Remember that your Quality Management System is a very practical and visible management system, so the auditor or appraiser will focus on results and talking to your staff.

Choosing a Poor Certification Body or Appraiser

It is not necessarily wise to choose the lowest priced certification body or appraiser. Remember the certification auditor or lead appraiser is there to find out what is working well and encourage you to get certified or rated, not to punish you for things you have not done, so it is in your own interest to find a competent certification body or appraiser. Do not just accept the lowest price! Remember, a Quality Management System, if implemented properly, can help you *reduce* cost.

Over-Documenting or Drowning In Detail

You can document absolutely everything that everyone does within an organization and basically back yourself into a corner. What you really want to document is the way your organization does certain things. Case in point—if you hire a welder to weld, you really should not have to implement a procedure or a process that discusses how they are supposed to perform general welding. Now, if there is something very specific to a customer or a contract requirement, then yes, you might want to document and implement a procedure that details that those things that are over and above what a general welder would do.

But you really do not need to document how to answer a phone. A receptionist should know how to answer a phone. If your organization has a specific way that you want the receptionist to answer phones, then yes, you would want to document and implement that procedure. This is a common trap that many organizations fall into. Come internal audit time, you may find that by over documenting you will make it virtually impossible for everyone in the organization to perform to those documents because you have over-documented everything and allowed no room for relatively inconsequential personal interpretations. Having processes and procedures in place, is a good thing. You just want to be very careful that you do not document yourself into a corner. Examples of over-documenting are having procedures or work instructions written for virtually everything, and overlap and repetition (including something in more than one procedure). An example of under-documenting would be where there is a lack of work instructions or procedures where the process affects the quality of the product or service.

Overly detailed documents can be convoluted and difficult to follow. Why say something in ten words when you can say it in one? I recommend using short sentences starting with a verb, avoiding using the passive voice in order to make it clear who is performing the task, and using white space for easy reading.

If you have a functional area or department that needs "artistic license" to do their work, or that deems their processes as "proprietary", you may encounter some resistance to documenting procedures. It is important to demonstrate to these functional areas that their documented processes will enable their work to be consistent and therefore measurable. The creativity takes place within the procedure. Document the procedure to describe the steps that must be followed, but not to prescribe the specific details that may be proprietary.

The Experts

One of the things that you can count on regardless of industry, it does not matter if it is automobile manufacturing or telecommunications, nuclear, pharmaceuticals, service industry, or IT, is that when you go to implement a Quality Management System there will be "experts". You will come across at least one or more people in your organization that at some point in their careers were a quality inspector or they had a course in ISO 9000 or CMMI, or they had some sort of quality training somewhere and now all of a sudden they believe they have excellent advice to offer. Most of them are trying to be helpful, but they have it in their mind that because they have had some exposure to quality, they know quality and they are going to help you, and they are going to tell you what you are doing wrong, and they will at some point (unless you possess the patience of a saint) drive you nuts! In some cases, it may be because they do not like having to do go through the implementation process, or their modest experience in quality was rather negative, so they are going to come at you with the intention of being a roadblock for you. Maybe their limited experience in quality or their training in quality was good, so now they truly believe they can be of assistance to you but what they do not understand is the big picture. If their experience or training is not very recent, the standards have probably changed. The industry has probably changed. The company's goals and business objectives are probably significantly different, so when they come at you with all of their unsolicited advice, they are actually getting in your way in most cases because of their limited perspective.

Thinking back over my career, I have yet to run into one of these people whose unsolicited advice or suggestions have actually been useful. Expect the "experts" to come out of the woodwork, but do not let them get in the way of your implementation project or get you down.

Chapter Nine

Was The Ride Worth The Price
Of The Ticket?

First, let us talk about consistency, reliability, and repeatability. For the purposes of this book and for implementing a Quality Management System, the definition of consistency would be reliability or uniformity of successive results or advance. In other words, you could say that a pitcher pitched with remarkable consistency throughout the season. With regard to repeatability, the definition would be to be able to do, experience, or produce again. In other words, repeat past successes. Considering reliability, the definition would be that trustworthiness to do what the system is expected or designed to do, or worthy of being depended upon. When your processes and procedures are consistent, you are able to take measurements against them. Those measurements will help you determine the reliability of your processes and procedures and therefore your products and services.

With regard to return on investment or ROI, a simple calculation (financial calculation) may not be enough for you to determine whether the ride was worth the price of the ticket in implementing a Quality Management System because there are several intangible benefits. However, I have included a sample ROI formula later in this chapter for calculation purposes so that you can see how much money you have invested versus the amount of sales dollars that winning new contracts or opening up your market place could increase.

Return on Investment (ROI)

Value is at the center of economic activity. Everyone—business or consumer—wants to get the greatest value they can for their money. Value is not always tangible, like a reliable schedule, a flashy car, or a good meal. The return on investment from your Quality Management System largely depends on how you implement and make use of the system–without proper strategic and measured investment; your chances of positive returns might be limited. When asked about expected return on investment from the implementation of CMMI, Kristine Titzer stated the following:

> My organization pursued a more structure Quality Management System as a distinguishing corporate characteristic to give them a competitive edge in the marketplace and ensure the consistency and quality of and satisfaction with deliverable products for current customers. The organization did not calculate ROI in a formula. ROI was demonstrated in a 100% re-compete win ratio and strategic and measured expansion of the organization over a ten-year period.

Cost of Quality (COQ)

In light of an increased focus on quality and customer satisfaction, senior managers have raised the question: Are Quality Management System-related efforts worth their cost? In other words, what is the return on investment? The answer to this question is unique for every organization and is based on two fundamental circumstances:

1. Quality must be measurable, preferably in dollars.
2. A cause-and-effect relationship needs to exist between quality and financial results.

Cost of quality is the amount of money an organization loses because its product or service was not done right in the first place. As my Uncle Dominic always said "It's a nickel more to go top shelf", meaning that if it only takes a few minutes more to do something right the first time, it is worth it. Organizations lose money every day due to poor quality. For most organizations, this can run from 15 to 30 percent of their total costs.

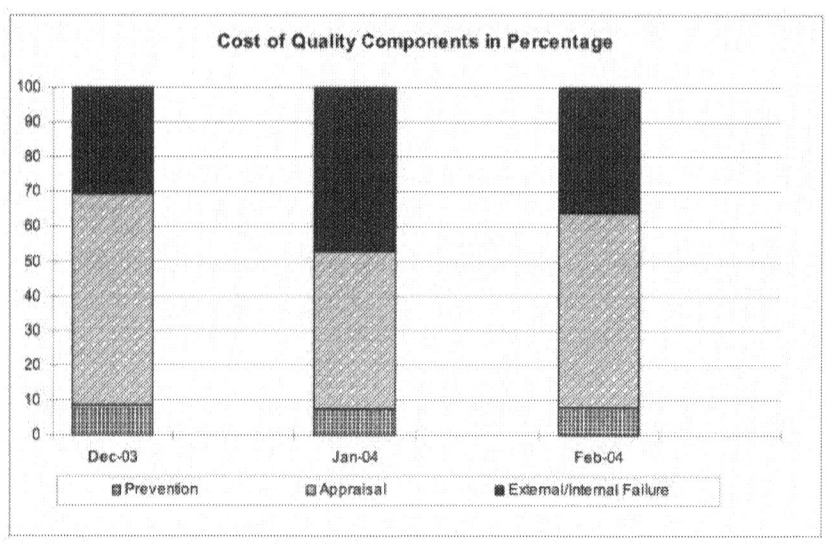

<u>Example of Types of Costs to Be Captured</u>

Appraisal
- Prototype inspection and test
- Supplier surveillance/audits
- Receiving inspection

External Failure and Internal Failure
- Field failures
- Purchasing change order
- Corrective action costs
- Rework
- Redesign
- Product Liability
- Scrap
- Design review
- Service after service

Prevention
- Drawing checks
- Supplier evaluations
- Specification reviews
- Specification changes
- Operation training
- Quality training
- Quality audits
- Preventive maintenance
- Process Capability Studies

Tangible ROI and Intangible ROI

With regard to what it was that prompted his organization to pursue implementing a Quality Management System, William Laramie stated, "In the competitive environment that exists, today for government contractors, any differentiator is an advantage. Quality is an integral aspect of project and program management and since this is one of our core business offerings it was crucial that we have a fully functioning Quality Management System."

According to the results of a study published by the SEI on March 4, 2005, the median Return on Investment (ROI) of organizations implementing process improvements through the use of CMMI models is 3:1. In addition, the organizations participating in the study reported a 38% reduction in project costs, a 50% improvement in schedule, a 14% increase in customer satisfaction, a 50% increase in productivity, and a 50% increase in quality.

While you may calculate a tangible financial ROI after you have implemented your Quality Management System, your larger ROI will predictably come from the intangibles such as increased customer satisfaction, faster time to market, greater employee efficiency etc. I have included a sample calculation for you as seen below:

$$\text{Simple ROI} = \frac{\text{Gains–Investment Costs}}{\text{Investment Costs}} = \frac{\$\,700,000 - \$500,000}{\$500,000} = 40\%$$

Simple ROI is the most frequently used form of ROI and the most easily understood.

With simple ROI, incremental gains from the investment are divided by the investment costs.

Richard Bechtold indicated the following with regard to ROI:

> We want reliable and predictable performance. Yet we also want flexibility and agility so that we can not only rapidly respond to opportunities, but also rapidly adapt to new priorities. Being reliable in core business capabilities is an excellent, if not essential, foundation for agile initiatives. Our return on investment is measured in terms of repeat customers and client engagements. Virtually all our customers and clients have returned to us for additional products and services.

He also stated that:

> Businesses want the option to compete for as much new business (or retain existing business) as they can profitably pursue. When quality goals (such as having a Quality Management System or ensuring quality standards compliance) are a precondition, businesses are highly motivated to achieve those goals. Additionally, many defense and other government agencies are adopting at least some 'business oriented' objectives so that they too can focus on 'return on investment' (ROI) targets, improved customer satisfaction, etc. The expected ROI for most client organizations is simply growth. They strive for more work and the additional resources to perform such work.

Chapter Ten

Ensuring the Ride Continues and Attracts New Visitors

Benchmarking

Benchmarking is the continuous process of measuring products, services, and practices against the strongest competitors or organizations recognized as leaders. Benchmarking is used by organizations searching for industry best practices that will lead to outstanding performance. It is only through a change of your current practices, or methods of performing your processes, that effectiveness can improve. Therefore, it is not good enough just to know that another organization is better at performing a certain activity–it is a matter of addressing the issues and learning from similar organizations on how to improve your processes.

Continuous Improvement

Continuous improvement is the type of change that is focused on increasing the effectiveness and/or efficiency of an organization to fulfill its policy and objectives. It is not limited to quality initiatives. Improvements in business strategies, business results, and customer, employee, and supplier relationships can be subject to continuous improvement. Continuous improvement should lead to better results such as price, cost, productivity, time to market, delivery, responsiveness, profit, and customer and employee satisfaction. In essence, it means 'getting better all the time'. Do not be afraid to make changes to your system. Simplify your documentation if need be.Do not expect the system to be perfect immediately, and get feedback from employees involved with your processes to initiate changes.

Registration to ISO 9000 or a CMMI rating should not be the end! You should continuously seek to improve the effectiveness and suitability of your Quality Management System through using:

1. Quality policy/plan
2. Quality objectives
3. Audit results
4. Analysis of data
5. Corrective and preventive actions
6. Lessons Learned
7. Management reviews

According to William Laramie, "the ability to capture lessons learned has improved our ability to review project and program performance and to learn both positive and negative aspects of like efforts." Richard Bechtold adds,

> Every organization intuitively knows it has room for improvement. People often think that process improvement is about achieving some state and then staying there. But that is wrong. Process improvement and Quality Management Systems are really about becoming very, very good at being able to change, and to rapidly adapt. Every organization intuitively knows it has room for improvement. People often think that process improvement is about achieving some state and then staying there. But that is wrong. Process improvement and Quality Management Systems are really about becoming very, very good at being able to change, and to rapidly adapt.

The Deming/Shewhart Cycle can be especially useful for you in resolving quality issues. The PDCA circle suggests continuous improvement by repeating the fundamental cycle of:
- <u>Plan</u> the improvement
  - o Get the data
  - o Analyze the problem

o Plan the solution
- <u>Do</u> the improvement
- <u>Check</u>—Measure the change, check the results, lessons learned
- <u>Act</u>—By adapting, adjusting or modifying the change as needed

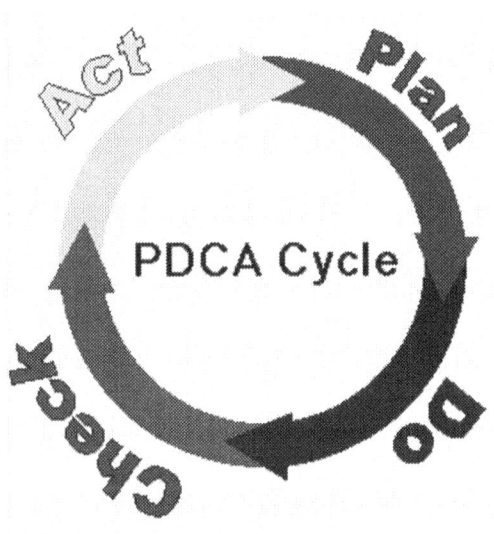

Over the course of time, products and/or services change, customers change, processes change, people change, suppliers change. Quality may change suddenly or deteriorate slowly. Serious problems need to be addressed as soon as they become evident. Cost and productivity also should be evaluated regularly. New technology, new suppliers, new processes, new scheduling techniques to accommodate the varying customer and industry changes, etc. may make cost and productivity improvements possible. Therefore, continuous improvement may not only resolve quality issues but may also be valuable in evaluating potential cost and/or productivity improvements. Use the system that you have built and implemented. Implement corrective actions. Emphasize the importance of Corrective Action, Management Reviews, and Internal Audits and continue training.

Lessons Learned

Gloria Redman suggests, "Any company contemplating CMMI certification should do it as early humanly possible. They need to do it in the very infancy of their company so they start out with the right processes in place and grow with those processes, and those processes grow with them. The lessons learned from implementation, from my standpoint are that if you wait too long to implement a Quality Management System, you have to take bad habits and try to replace them with good habits. It would be better not to have to replace any habits and have a very good process already in place, which you would have if you pursued the implementation of a Quality Management System early on and maintained it and endeavored for continuous improvement."

William Laramie offers the following advice to organizations endeavoring to implement a Quality Management System:

> Up and until the publication of this book, there was no definitive source to turn to in order to evaluate the pros and cons of implementing a Quality Management System for small business. Much of the material published has been prepared by organizations seeking to sell services for the implementation of the Quality Management System. This book provides a roadmap of questions to ask.
>
> I would advise organizations seeking to undertake a Quality Management System effort to plan, plan, plan. First, there will be an impact to culture. The typical issues facing many small businesses to seek work and perform and to worry about the infrastructure at a future date. As employees performing, the typical corporate functions seek to fulfill the needs of their employees performing contracted services, the processes and procedures normally lag behind and as a result the, 'it's always been done this way,' becomes the accepted answer whenever an internal practice or procedure is challenged. Quality Management System drives standardization and challenges the status quo. This is an unsettling event for many who have formed habits, which may or may not be truly beneficial to the organization. Once employees understand the need for change, can see a tangible benefit (i.e., it can reduce rework, frustration in finding the right form, and standardizing activities), and understand the nature and direction the organization is going as it embraces Quality Management System the change occurs. As is pointed out in this book, it is a roller coaster ride that ends with a sense of accomplishment.

The quality ride is a continuous ride…never-ending!

Glossary of Terms

CMMI Related Glossary

Acceptance criteria
The criteria that a product or product component must satisfy to be accepted by a user, customer, or other authorized entity.

Acceptance testing
Formal testing conducted to enable a user, customer, or other authorized entity to determine whether to accept a product or product component. (See "unit testing".)

Achievement profile
In the continuous representation, a list of process areas and their corresponding capability levels that represent the organization's progress for each process area while advancing through the capability levels. (See "target staging," "capability level profile"and"target profile.")

Acquisition
The process of obtaining, through contract, any discrete action or proposed action by the acquisition entity that would commit to invest (appropriated funds) for obtaining products and services.

Advanced practices
In the continuous representation, all the specific practices with a capability level of two or higher.

Agreement/contract requirements
All technical and non-technical requirements related to an acquisition.

Allocated requirement
Requirement that levies all or part of the performance and functionality of a higher-level requirement on a lower level architectural element or design component.

Alternative practice
A practice that is a substitute for one or more generic or specific practices contained in CMMI models that achieves an equivalent effect toward satisfying the generic or specific goal associated with model practices. Alternative practices are not necessarily one-for-one replacements for the generic or specific practices.

Appraisal findings
The conclusions of an appraisal that identify the most important issues, problems, or opportunities within the appraisal scope. Findings include, at a minimum, strengths and weaknesses based on valid observations.

Appraisal participants
Members of the organizational unit who participate in providing information during the appraisal.

Appraisal rating
As used in CMMI appraisal materials, the value assigned by an appraisal team to either (1) a CMMI goal or process area, (2) the capability level of a process area, or (3) the maturity level of an organizational unit. The rating is determined by enacting the defined rating process for the appraisal method being employed.

Appraisal reference model
As used in CMMI appraisal materials, the CMMI model to which an appraisal team correlates implemented process activities.

Appraisal scope
The definition of the boundaries of the appraisal encompassing the organizational limits and the CMMI model limits.

Assignable cause of process variation
In CMMI, the term "special cause of process variation" is used in place of "assignable cause of process variation" to ensure consistency. Both terms are defined identically. (See "special cause of process variation".)

Audit
In CMMI process-improvement work, an independent examination of a work product or set of work products to determine whether requirements are being met.

Base measure
A distinct property or characteristic of an entity and the method for quantifying it. (See "derived measures".)

Base practices
In the continuous representation, all the specific practices with a capability level of 1.

Baseline
(See "configuration baseline", "process performance baseline", and "product baseline".)

Capability evaluation
An appraisal by a trained team of professionals used as a discriminator to select suppliers, for contract monitoring, or for incentives. Evaluations are used to help decision makers make better acquisition decisions, improve subcontractor performance, and provide insight to a purchasing organization.

Capability maturity model
A capability maturity model (CMM) contains the essential elements of effective processes for one or more disciplines. It also describes an evolutionary improvement path from ad hoc, immature processes to disciplined, mature processes with improved quality and effectiveness.

Causal analysis
The analysis of defects to determine their cause.

Change management
Judicious use of means to effect a change, or proposed change, on a product or service. (See "configuration management".)

Common cause of process variation
The variation of a process that exists because of normal and expected interactions among the components of a process. (See "special cause of process variation".)

Configuration audit
An audit conducted to verify that a configuration item conforms to a specified standard or requirement. (See "audit" and "configuration item".)

Configuration baseline

The configuration information formally designated at a specific time during a product's or product component's life. Configuration baselines, plus approved changes from those baselines, constitute the current configuration information. (See "product life cycle".)

Configuration control

An element of configuration management consisting of the evaluation, coordination, approval or disapproval, and implementation of changes to configuration items after formal establishment of their configuration identification. (See "configuration management", "configuration identification," and "configuration item".)

Configuration control board

A group of people responsible for evaluating and approving or disapproving proposed changes to configuration items, and for ensuring implementation of approved changes. (See "configuration item".) Configuration control boards are also known as "change control boards".

Configuration identification

An element of configuration management consisting of selecting the configuration items for a product, assigning unique identifiers to them, and recording their functional and physical characteristics in technical documentation. (See "configuration management," "configuration item," and "product.")

Configuration item

An aggregation of work products that is designated for configuration management and treated as a single entity in the configuration management process. (See "configuration management.")

Configuration management

A discipline applying technical and administrative direction and surveillance to (1) identify and document the functional and physical characteristics of a configuration item, (2) control changes to those characteristics, (3) record and report change processing and implementation status, and (4) verify compliance with specified requirements. [IEEE STD 610.1990] (See "configuration identification," "configuration control," "configuration status accounting," and "configuration audit.")

Configuration status accounting

An element of configuration management consisting of the recording and reporting of information needed to manage a configuration effectively. This information includes a listing of the approved configuration identification, the status of proposed changes to the configuration, and the implementation status of approved changes. (See "configuration management" and "configuration identification.")

Continuous representation

A capability maturity model structure wherein capability levels provide a recommended order for approaching process improvement within each specified process area. (See "staged representation," "capability level," and "process area.")

Corrective action

Acts or deeds used to remedy a situation, remove an error, or adjust a condition.

COTS

Items that can be purchased from a commercial vendor. (COTS stands for "commercial off the shelf.")

Data management

Principles, processes, and systems for the sharing and management of data.

Derived measures

Data resulting from the mathematical function of two or more base measures. (See "base measure.")

Derived requirements

Requirements that are not explicitly stated in the customer requirements, but are inferred (1) from contextual requirements (e.g., applicable standards, laws, policies, common practices, and management decisions), or (2) from requirements needed to specify a product component. Derived requirements can also arise during analysis and design of components of the product or system. (See "product requirements.")

Entry criteria

States of being that must be present before an effort can begin successfully.

Equivalent staging
Equivalent staging is a target staging, created using the continuous representation that is defined so that the results of using the target staging can be compared to the maturity levels of the staged representation. (See "target staging," "maturity level," "capability level profile," and "target profile.") Such staging permits benchmarking of progress among organizations, enterprises, and projects, regardless of the CMMI representation used. The organization may implement components of CMMI models beyond those reported as part of equivalent staging. Equivalent staging is only a measure to relate how the organization is compared to other organizations in terms of maturity levels.

Exit criteria
States of being that must be present before an effort can end successfully.

Functional analysis
Examination of a defined function to identify all the sub-functions necessary to the accomplishment of that function; identification of functional relationships and interfaces (internal and external) and capturing these in a functional architecture; and flow down of upper level performance requirements and assignment of these requirements to lower level sub-functions. (See "functional architecture.")

Functional architecture
The hierarchical arrangement of functions, their internal and external (external to the aggregation itself) functional interfaces and external physical interfaces, their respective functional and performance requirements, and their design constraints.

Institutionalization
The ingrained way of doing business that an organization follows routinely as part of its corporate culture.

Integrated team
A group of people with complementary skills and expertise who are committed to delivering specified work products in timely collaboration. Integrated team members provide skills and advocacy appropriate to all phases of the work products' life and are collectively responsible for delivering the work products as specified. An integrated team should include empowered representatives from organizations, disciplines, and functions that have a stake in the success of the work products.

Interface control
In configuration management, the process of (1) identifying all functional and physical characteristics relevant to the interfacing of two or more configuration items provided by one or more organizations, and (2) ensuring that the proposed changes to these characteristics are evaluated and approved prior to implementation. (See "configuration management" and "configuration item.")

Life-cycle model
A partitioning of the life of a product into phases that guide the project from identifying customer needs through product retirement.

Maturity level
Degree of process improvement across a predefined set of process areas in which all goals within the set are attained. (See "capability level" and "process area.")

Memorandum of agreement (moa)
Binding documents of understanding or agreements between two or more parties. (Also known as a "memorandum of understanding.")

Objective evidence
As used in CMMI appraisal materials, qualitative or quantitative information, records, or statements of fact pertaining to the characteristics of an item or service or to the existence and implementation of a process element, which are based on observation, measurement, or test and which are verifiable.

Objectively evaluate
To review activities and work products against criteria that minimizes subjectivity and bias by the reviewer. An example of an objective evaluation is an audit against requirements, standards, or procedures by an independent quality assurance function. (See "audit.")

Observation
As used in CMMI appraisal materials, a written record that represents the appraisal team members' understanding of information either seen or heard during the appraisal data collection activities. The written record may take the form of a statement or may take alternative forms as long as the information content is preserved.

Organization's business objectives

Senior-management-developed strategies designed to ensure an organization's continued existence and enhance its profitability, market share, and other factors influencing the organization's success. (See "quantitative objective" and "quality and process-performance objectives.") Such objectives may include reducing the number of change requests during a system's integration phase, reducing development cycle time, increasing the number of errors found in a product's first or second phase of development, reducing the number of customer-reported defects, etc., when applied to systems-engineering activities.

Organizational maturity

The extent to which an organization has explicitly and consistently deployed processes that are documented, managed, measured, controlled, and continuously improved. Organizational maturity may be measured via appraisals.

Organizational policy

A guiding principle typically established by senior management that is adopted by an organization to influence and determine decisions.

Organizational unit

That part of an organization that is the subject of an appraisal (also known as the organizational scope of the appraisal).an organizational unit deploys one or more processes that have a coherent process context and operates within a coherent set of business objectives. An organizational unit is typically part of a larger organization, although in a small organization, the organizational unit may be the whole organization.

Process asset

Anything that the organization considers useful in attaining the goals of a process area. (See "organizational process assets.")

Process attribute

A measurable characteristic of process capability applicable to any process.

Process capability

The range of expected results that can be achieved by following a process.

Process group

A collection of specialists that facilitate the definition, maintenance, and improvement of the process (es) used by the organization.

Process improvement
A program of activities designed to improve the performance and maturity of the organization's processes, and the results of such a program.

Process owner
The person (or team) responsible for defining and maintaining a process. At the organizational level, the process owner is the person (or team) responsible for the description of a standard process; at the project level, the process owner is the person (or team) responsible for the description of the defined process. A process may therefore have multiple owners at different levels of responsibility. (See "standard process" and "defined process.")

Process performance
A measure of actual results achieved by following a process. It is characterized by both process measures (e.g., effort, cycle time, and defect removal efficiency) and product measures (e.g., reliability, defect density, and response time).

Process performance baseline
A documented characterization of the actual results achieved by following a process, which is used as a benchmark for comparing actual process performance against expected process performance. (See "process performance.")

Process tailoring
To make, alter, or adapt a process description for a particular end. For example, a project tailors its defined process from the organization's set of standard processes to meet the objectives, constraints, and environment of the project. (See "process description," "organization's set of standard processes," and "defined process.")

Product-component requirements
Product-component requirements provide a complete specification of a product component, including fit, form, function, performance, and any other requirement.

Product-related life-cycle processes
Processes associated with a product throughout one or more phases of its life (i.e., from conception through disposal), such as the manufacturing and support processes.

Product requirements
A refinement of the customer requirements into the developers' language, making implicit requirements into explicit derived requirements. (See "product-component requirements" and "derived requirements.") The developer uses the product requirements to guide the design and building of the product.

Program
(1) A project. (2) A collection of related projects and the infrastructure that supports them, including objectives, methods, activities, plans, and success measures. (See "project.")

Project progress and performance
What a project achieves with respect to implementing project plans, including effort, cost, schedule, and technical performance.

Quality
The ability of a set of inherent characteristics of a product, product component, or process to fulfill requirements of customers.

Quality assurance
A planned and systematic means for assuring management that defined standards, practices, procedures, and methods of the process are applied.

Quality control
The operational techniques and activities that are used to fulfill requirements for quality.

Quantitative objective
Desired target value expressed as quantitative measures. (See "quality and process-performance objectives" and "process-improvement objectives.")

Reference model
A model that is used as a benchmark for measuring some attribute.

Required CMMI components
CMMI components that are essential to achieving process improvement in a given process area. These components are used in appraisals to determine process capability. Specific goals and generic goals are required model components.

Requirement

(1) A condition or capability needed by a user to solve a problem or achieve an objective. (2) a condition or capability that must be met or possessed by a product or product component to satisfy a contract, standard, specification, or other formally imposed documents. (3) A documented representation of a condition or capability as in (1) or (2).

Requirements analysis

The determination of product-specific performance and functional characteristics based on analyses of customer needs, expectations, and constraints; operational concept; projected utilization environments for people, products, and processes; and measures of effectiveness.

Requirements elicitation

Using systematic techniques, like prototypes and structured surveys, to proactively identify and document customer and end-user needs.

Requirements management

The management of all requirements received by or generated by the project, including both technical and non-technical requirements as well as those requirements levied on the project by the organization.

Requirements traceability

The evidence of an association between a requirement and its source requirement, its implementation, and its verification.

Return on investment

The ratio of revenue from output (product) to production costs, which determines whether an organization benefits from performing an action to produce something.

Risk analysis

The evaluation, classification, and prioritization of risks.

Risk identification

An organized, thorough approach to seek out probable or realistic risks in achieving objectives.

Risk management
An organized, analytic process to identify what might cause harm or loss (identify risks), assess and quantify the identified risks, and to develop and, if needed, implement an appropriate approach to prevent or handle risk causes that could result in significant harm or loss.

Root cause
A root cause is a source of a defect such that if it is removed, the defect is decreased or removed.

Stable process
The state in which all special causes of process variation have been removed and prevented from recurring so that only the common causes of process variation of the process remain. (See "special cause of process variation," "common cause of variation," "standard process," "statistically managed process," and "capable process.")

Staged representation
A model structure wherein attaining the goals of a set of process areas establishes a maturity level; each level builds a foundation for subsequent levels. (See "process area" and "maturity level.")

Standard process
An operational definition of the basic process that guides the establishment of a common process in an organization. A standard process describes the fundamental process elements that are expected to be incorporated into any defined process. It also describes the relationships (e.g., ordering and interfaces) between these process elements. (See terminology for an explanation of how "defined process" is used in the CMMI product suite.)

Statement of work (sow)
A description of contracted work required to complete a project.

Statistical predictability
The performance of a quantitative process that is controlled using statistical and other quantitative techniques.

Statistical process control
Statistically based analysis of a process and measurements of process performance, which will identify common and special causes of variation in the process performance, and maintain process performance within limits.

Supplier
(1) An entity delivering products or performing services being acquired. (2) an individual, partnership, company, corporation, association, or other service having an agreement (contract) with an acquirer for the design, development, manufacture, maintenance, modification, or supply of items under the terms of an agreement (contract).

Systems engineering
The interdisciplinary approach governing the total technical and managerial effort required to transform a set of customer needs, expectations, and constraints into a product solution and support that solution throughout the product's life. This includes the definition of technical performance measures, the integration of engineering specialties towards the establishment of a product architecture, and the definition of supporting life-cycle processes that balance cost, performance, and schedule objectives.

Target profile
In the continuous representation, a list of process areas and their corresponding capability levels that represent an objective for process improvement. (See "capability level profile" and "achievement profile.")

Target staging
In the continuous representation, a sequence of target profiles that describes the path of process improvement to be followed by the organization. (See "capability level profile," "achievement profile," and "target profile.")

Technical requirements
Properties (attributes) of products or services to be acquired or developed.

Verifying implementation
A common feature of CMMI model process areas with a staged representation that groups the generic practices related to review by higher-level management, and objective evaluation of conformance to process descriptions, procedures, and standards.

Version control
The establishment and maintenance of baselines and the identification of changes to baselines that make it possible to return to the previous baseline.

Weakness
As used in CMMI appraisal materials, the ineffective, or lack of, implementation of one or more CMMI model practices.

Work breakdown structure
An arrangement of work elements and their relationship to each other and to the end product.

Work product and task attributes
Characteristics of products, services, and project tasks used to help in estimating project work. These characteristics include items such as size, complexity, weight, form, fit, or function. They are typically used as one input to deriving other project and resource estimates (e.g., effort, cost, schedule).

General Quality Related Glossary

Accreditation
Certification by a duly recognized body of the facilities, capability, objectivity, competence, and integrity of an agency, service or operational group or individual to provide the specific service(s) or operation(s) needed.

ANSI
American National Standards Institute

AS9100
Quality system requirements for suppliers to the aerospace industry (previously known as AS9000).

ASQ
American Society for Quality

Assessment
An evaluation process including a document review, an on-site audit and an analysis and report. (See Quality audit)

Audit
Systematic, independent, and documented process for obtaining audit evidence and evaluating it objectively to determine the extent to which audit criteria are fulfilled.

Audit client
Organization or person requesting an audit.

Audit conclusion
Outcome of an audit provided by the audit team after consideration of the audit objectives and all audit findings.

Audit criteria
Set of policies, procedures or requirements used as a reference (while conducting an audit).

Auditee
Organization being audited.

Audit evidence
Records, statements of fact or other information, which are relevant to the audit criteria and verifiable.

Audit findings
Results of the evaluation of the collected audit evidence against audit criteria.

Auditor
Person with the competence to conduct an audit.

Audit program
Set of one or more audits planned for a specific time frame and directed towards a specific purpose.

Audit team
One or more auditors conducting an audit.

Average or mean
The most common expression of the centering of a distribution. It is calculated by totaling the observed values and dividing by the number of observations.

Benchmark Data
The results of an investigation to determine how competitors and/or best-in-class companies achieve their level of performance.

Certification
The procedure and action by a duly authorized body of determining, verifying, and attesting in writing to the qualifications of personnel, processes, procedures, or items in accordance with applicable requirements.

Competence
Demonstrated ability to apply knowledge skills.

Compliance
An affirmative indication or judgment that the supplier of a product or service has met the requirements of the relevant specifications, contract, or regulation; also the state of meeting the requirements.

Conformance
An affirmative indication or judgment that a product or service has met the requirements of the relevant specifications, contract, or regulation; also the state of meeting the requirements.

Conformity
Fulfillment of a requirement.

Continuous improvement
Recurring activity to increase the ability to fulfill requirements.

Correction
Action to eliminate a detected nonconformity.

Corrective action
Action to eliminate the cause of a detected nonconformity or other undesirable situation.

Customer
Organization or person that receives a product.

Customer satisfaction
Customer's perception of the degree to which the customer's requirements have been fulfilled.

Defect
Non-fulfillment of a requirement related to an intended or specified use.

Design and development
Set of processes that transforms requirements into specified characteristics or into the specification of a product, process or system.

Design input
The physical and performance requirements of a device that are used as a basis for device design.

Design Review
A formal, documented, comprehensive, and systematic examination of a design to evaluate the design requirements and the capability of the design to meet these requirements and to identify problems and propose solutions.

Design Validation
Testing to ensure that product conforms to defined user needs and/or requirements. Design validation follows successful design verification and is normally performed on the final product under defined operating conditions. Multiple validations may be performed if there are different intended uses.

Detection or inspection
A past-oriented strategy that attempts to identify unacceptable output after it has been produced and separate it from the good output.

Distribution
The population (universe) from which observations are drawn, categorized into cells, and form identifiable patterns. It is based on the concept of variation that states that anything measured repeatedly will arrive at different results. These results will fall into statistically predictable patterns. A bell-shaped curve (normal distribution) is an example of a distribution in which the greatest number of observations occur in the center with fewer and fewer observations falling evenly on either side of the average.

Efficiency
Relationship between the result achieved and the resources used.

Effectiveness
Extent to which planned activities are realized and planned results achieved.

Infrastructure (of an organization)
System of facilities, equipment, and services needed for the operation of an organization.

Inspection
Conformity evaluation by observation and judgement accompanied as appropriate by measurement, testing or gauging.

Interested party
Person or group having an interest in the performance or success of an organization.

ISO
International Organization for Standardization

ISO 9000
International Standard for Quality Systems

Kaizen
Taken from the Japanese words kai and zen, where kai means change and zen means good. The popular meaning is continuous improvement of all areas of a company not just quality.

Management system
System to establish policy and objectives and to achieve those objectives.

Measurement control system
Set of interrelated or interacting elements necessary to achieve metrological confirmation and continuous control of measurement processes.

MRB
Material review board

NIST
National Institute of Science and Technology

Nonconformance
Product or material, which does not conform to the customer requirements or specifications.

Nonconformity
A process, which does not conform to a quality system requirement.

Objective evidence
Data supporting the existence or verity of something,

Organization
Group of people and facilities with an arrangement of responsibilities, authorities, and relationships.

Organizational structure
Arrangement of responsibilities, authorities, and relationships between people.

Preventive action
Action to eliminate the cause of a potential nonconformity or other undesirable potential situation.

Procedure
Specified way to carry out an activity or a process.

Process
Set of interrelated or interacting activities, which transforms inputs into outputs.

Process quality audit
An analysis of elements of a process and appraisal of completeness, correctness of conditions, and probable effectiveness.

Process validation
Establishing by objective evidence that a process consistently produces a result or product meeting its predetermined specifications.

Product quality audit
A quantitative assessment of conformance to required product characteristics.

Project
Unique process, consisting of a set of coordinated and controlled activities with start and finish dates, undertaken to achieve an objective conforming to specific requirements, including the constraints of time, cost, and resources.

QMS
Quality Management System

Quality
Degree to which a set of inherent (existing) characteristics fulfils requirements.

Quality assurance
Part of quality management focused on providing confidence that quality requirements will be fulfilled. Prevents nonconformances

Quality audit (also quality assessment, or conformity assessment)
A systematic and independent examination and evaluation to determine whether quality activities and results comply with planned arrangements and whether these arrangements are implemented effectively and are suitable to achieve objectives.

Quality control
Part of quality management focused on fulfilling quality requirements. Detects nonconformances

Quality engineering
That branch of engineering which deals with the principles and practice of product and service quality assurance and control.

Quality improvement
Part of quality management focused on increasing the ability to fulfill quality requirements.

Quality management
Coordinated activities to direct and control an organization with regard to quality.

Quality Management System
Management system to direct and control an organization with regard to quality.

Quality manual
Document specifying the Quality Management System of an organization.

Quality measure
A quantitative measure of the features and characteristics of a product or service.

Quality objective
Something sought, or aimed for, related to quality.

Quality plan
Document specifying which procedures and associated resources shall be applied by whom and when to a specific project, product, process or contract.

Quality policy
Overall intentions and direction of an organization related to quality as formally expressed by top management.

Quality system
The organizational structure, responsibilities, procedures, processes, and resources for implementing quality management.

Quality system audit
A documented activity performed to verify, by examination and evaluation of objective evidence, that applicable elements of the quality system are suitable and have been developed, documented, and effectively implemented in accordance with specified requirements.

Realization (as used in ISO 9000:2000)
The carrying out of an action or process to completion.

Record
Document stating results achieved or providing evidence of activities performed.

Registrar
A company that conducts quality system assessments to the Quality System Requirements.

Reliability
The probability that an item will continue to function at customer expectation levels at a measurement point, under specified environmental and duty cycle conditions.

Repair
Action taken on nonconforming product so that the product will fulfill the intended usage although the product may not conform to the original requirements.

Requirement
Need or expectation that is stated, generally implied, or obligatory.

Review
Activity undertaken to determine the suitability, adequacy, and effectiveness of the subject matter to achieve established objectives.

Rework
Action taken on a nonconforming product so that it will fulfill the specified requirements before it is released for distribution.

Scrap
Action on a nonconforming product to preclude its originally intended use.

Six Sigma
Quality process, developed at Motorola, focused on reducing defects to a six sigma level (3.4 defects per million parts; 0.00034%), for all practical purposes zero defects.

Specification
The document that prescribes the requirements with which the product or service has to conform.

Stakeholder
An individual or group of individuals with a common interest in the performance of the supplier organization and the environment in which it operates.

Supplier
Organization or person that provides a product.

System
Set of interrelated or interacting elements.

Technical expert (in an audit)
Person who provides specific knowledge of or expertise on the subject to be audited.

TL 9000
Quality system requirements for suppliers to the telecommunications industry

Top management
Person or group of people who direct and control an organization at the highest level.

TQM
Total quality management

Traceability
Ability to trace the history, application, or location of that which is under consideration.

Validation
Confirmation, through the provision of objective evidence, that the requirements for a specific intended use or application have been fulfilled.

Verification
Confirmation, through the provision of objective evidence, that specified requirements have been fulfilled.

Waiver
Written authorization to use or release a quantity of material, components, or stores already manufactured but not conforming to the specified requirements.

Zero Defects
The quality concept of zero tolerance for defects (see Six Sigma)

References

Project Management Institute's *Project Management Body of Knowledge*® (PMBOK®)

ISO 9001:2000 Quality Management Systems—Requirements

CMMI-SE/SW/IPPD/SS, V1.1 *Capability Maturity Model*® *Integration (CMMI* *SM)*, Version 1.1

Deming, WE "The New Economics: for industry, government, education." 1994 MIT CAES, Cambridge

Benchmarking: The Search for Industry Best Practices That Lead to Superior Performance by Robert Camp (1989, ASQC Press)

Transitioning to CMMI: A Guide for Executives, Version 0.51, April 2002

"CMMI Performance Results", http://www.sei.cmu.edu/CMMI/results/results-by-category.html

Demonstrating the Impact and Benefits of CMMI®: An Update and Preliminary Results, Dennis R. Goldenson and Diane L. Gibson, Carnegie Mellon Software Engineering Institute, CMU/SEI-2003-SR-009, October 2003.

Index

978-0-595-40194-9
0-595-40194-5

www.ingramcontent.com/pod-product-compliance
Lightning Source LLC
Chambersburg PA
CBHW030852180526
45163CB00004B/1537